PSYCHOLOGY LIBRARY EDITIONS:
COMPARATIVE PSYCHOLOGY

Volume 1

ANIMAL PSYCHOLOGY

ANIMAL PSYCHOLOGY
Its Nature and its Problems

J.A. BIERENS DE HAAN

Routledge
Taylor & Francis Group

LONDON AND NEW YORK

First published in 1948 by Hutchinson & Co.

This edition first published in 2018
by Routledge
2 Park Square, Milton Park, Abingdon, Oxon OX14 4RN

and by Routledge
711 Third Avenue, New York, NY 10017

Routledge is an imprint of the Taylor & Francis Group, an informa business

British Library Cataloguing in Publication Data
A catalogue record for this book is available from the British Library

ISBN: 978-1-138-50329-8 (Set)
ISBN: 978-1-351-12878-0 (Set) (ebk)
ISBN: 978-0-8153-6936-3 (Volume 1) (hbk)
ISBN: 978-0-8153-6937-0 (Volume 1) (pbk)
ISBN: 978-1-351-25254-6 (Volume 1) (ebk)

Publisher's Note
The publisher has gone to great lengths to ensure the quality of this reprint but points out that some imperfections in the original copies may be apparent.

Disclaimer
The publisher has made every effort to trace copyright holders and would welcome correspondence from those they have been unable to trace.

ANIMAL PSYCHOLOGY

Its Nature and its Problems

by

Dr. J. A. BIERENS DE HAAN,
C.M.Z.S.

SECRETARY OF THE DUTCH SOCIETY
OF SCIENCES. LATE LECTURER IN
EXPERIMENTAL ZOOLOGY IN THE
UNIVERSITY OF AMSTERDAM.

HUTCHINSON'S UNIVERSITY LIBRARY
47 Princes Gate, London
New York   *Melbourne*   **Sydney**   *Cape Town*

THIS VOLUME IS NUMBER 15 IN
HUTCHINSON'S UNIVERSITY LIBRARY

Printed in Great Britain by
Burrow's Press Ltd.,
Cheltenham and London.

H 2004

CONTENTS

PREFACE

T H E reader will not expect to find in the pages of a book of such a modest size as this a full account of all facts known in the field of animal psychology and of all theories built on these facts. The author has rather preferred to follow, and to work out, one particular line of thought, to wit : the idea that the instincts, as they are defined on page 38 of this book, are the spring and basis of all animal behaviour (with the exception perhaps of play), and therewith the core of the animal's mind, and that individual experience, gathered by the animal in the course of its life, may influence and reconstruct these instincts, so as to guide, in the form of intelligence and understanding, this behaviour along new (i.e., not innate) paths. Thus, instinct and experience become the pillars upon which animal behaviour is built up ; instinct, intelligence, and understanding form a triad round which the facts of the psychology of animals may be grouped. As a foundation of all this the author first tries to prove the good right of a real and genuine animal psychology, not hampered by objectivistic and behaviouristic scruples, while in a final chapter, by way of conclusion, he tries to give an image of how the world of the animal is built up. Along this road the reader will meet the principal facts of animal psychology and, for the rest, may add to them by studying some of the works mentioned at the close of this volume. The author expresses the hope that this way of treatment may serve its purpose and form an introduction to the fascinating science of the psychology of animals.

Amsterdam, Christmas 1946.

CHAPTER I

THE PROBLEM OF ANIMAL PSYCHOLOGY

Tschuang-Tse and Hui-Tse were standing on the bridge across the Hao river. Tschuang-Tse said : "Look how the minnows are shooting to and fro ! That is the joy of the fishes."

"You are not a fish," said Hui-Tse, "how can you know in what the joy of the fishes consists ?"

"You are not I," answered Tschuang-Tse, "how can you know I do not know in what the joy of the fishes consists ?"

"I am not you," Hui-Tse conceded, "and I do not know you. All I know is that you are not a fish ; therefore you cannot know the fishes."

Tschuang-Tse answered : "Let us return to your question. You ask me : 'How can you know in what the joy of the fishes consists ?' Essentially you knew that I know, and yet you asked me. No matter : I know it from my own joy of the water."

The old Chinese Tschuang-Tse.
(Quoted after Hempelmann.)

WHOEVER for some moments has attentively watched the behaviour of an animal, be it that of his dog who accompanied him on a walk through the fields, or of a blackbird singing in his garden, or even of an ant going along an ant-path in the wood, will undoubtedly have felt the question arise in him : What are the springs of that animal activity ? Why does that dog suddenly start barking under that tree ; why does that bird suddenly fly away ; why does that ant all at once turn back, while there is no perceptible reason why it should not go straight on ? And, further, what is the nature of these springs of activity ? Are the actions of animals purely mechanical by nature, and is the animal, therefore, wholly comparable to a finely constructed machine, differing from a motor-car or musical-box only in that it is born and feeds itself and dies when its time has come ? Or are their actions built up from an integration of reflexes, of the same nature as the contraction of our pupil when light falls on the eye, or the secretion of the glands of our stomach when we see or taste food, vital phenomena indeed, but occurring beyond a consciousness that experiences them ? Or may we admit that the animal in his actions is guided by something comparable to the inner experiences that underlie our own deeds ; by feelings, perceptions, desires, perhaps even by understanding and judgment ? Mostly the spectator disposes of all these questions by saying that the animal is driven to its actions by its "instinct," not worrying very much about the import he has to give to this concept. But, as it is said that curiosity may be regarded as the mother of all science, so interest in the behaviour of animals may certainly be regarded as the origin of the science of animal psychology.

Not everybody, however, who meditates on the nature of animal activity, has by this fact alone the right to term himself an animal psychologist. There are, as we saw just now, three main ways of explaining this activity. The first is, to regard the animal as a living machine and to explain its actions as the outcome of purely mechanical causation. The prototype of this view in modern times is found in the conceptions of Descartes. Descartes distinguished two fundamentally different realities or "substances" : a material one, the "*Substantia extensa*," characterized by its extensiveness, and a spiritual one, the "*Substantia cogitans*," characterized by a self-conscious thinking. As a result of this distinction he admitted an extreme dualism of body and mind. The body, as a part of the *Substantia extensa*, to him was nothing but an ingeniously constructed machine, whereas the mind, because of its faculty of thinking, was part of the *Substantia cogitans*. Now the animals, as they do not speak and never make gestures as we do when we wish to express our thoughts, in his opinion do not think and therefore have no minds and are nothing but such machines—machines suited to the purpose for which they were constructed, but, in spite of their often seemingly intelligent behaviour, wholly corresponding to our watches and clocks, which are built up only of wheels and springs and yet measure the time better than we do. It will be clear that in such conceptions there is no place for real animal psychology.

There will probably not be many people who nowadays share Descartes' views, at least as far as the higher animals are concerned. But as regards the lower kinds of animal the case is somewhat different. It was only at the beginning of this century that Loeb, in his *Theory of Tropisms*, declared that the actions of animals were nothing but the direct effect of external forces, such as light, gravity, heat, and the like, on the bodies of these animals. These forces, being of a purely physico-chemical nature, worked in a way quite independent of the will of the animal, and were wholly comparable in their workings with that of a magnet on iron filings, or that of gravity on the movement of celestial bodies. Although Loeb's ideas have lost their influence through severe criticism from different sides, I am not sure that their after-effects do not still confuse the minds of some students. At any rate Loeb does not bring us nearer to animal psychology than Descartes did.

The case is somewhat different when we come to a second way of explaining animal activity, to wit, the physiological one. The man who adopts this physiological way of explanation, that is, the man who tries to analyse the actions of animals into physiological stimulation of sense-organs and nerves, the contractions of muscles and secretion of glands, may have two reasons for doing so. First, he may be a professional physiologist, who need not concern himself about any other aspects of animal activity. In this he is certainly in his right, and we may respect his attitude as long as he is consistent and does not try to make us believe that what he gives us is a kind of psychology. Physiology and psychology, it may be said here by the way, are two wholly different branches of science, however many points of contact they may have. The former occupies itself with the material phenomena of sense stimulations, nerve impulses, secretions and kindred phenomena, the latter with psychical phenomena, such as sensations and perceptions, feelings and emotions, desires and memories, and the like. A confusion of the aims of two so different branches of science has never led to a clearer understanding, and certainly this is not the case with physiology and psychology. Besides, this physiological attitude in the explanation of animal activity is sometimes adopted not only by the professional physiologist but also by people who for some theoretical reason believe it to be the only possible or satisfactory one. We will come back later on to this attitude. Anyhow, this physiological explanation does not bring us to any real psychology of the animals either.

The third way of explaining animal behaviour, and the only one that leads to real psychology of animals is, as we have already indicated, that of explaining it in terms of psychic phenomena, of trying to find out the psychic phenomena that underlie their behaviour. What, then, are these psychic phenomena? They are phenomena we experience in ourselves as immaterial and not occurring in space (as do the physiological processes in our body) phenomena we know more directly than any other phenomenon on earth, and know directly in ourselves alone. Our own visual or auditory sensations, our own perceptions of the world around us, our own feelings of joy or misery, our own desires and strivings, are phenomena we experience more directly than we do the trees in our garden or the flow of a river ; on the other hand we have to admit that the corresponding inner experiences of other men remain a closed book to us, as long as they do not reveal them to us by some way of communication. The most direct knowledge of our own, a fundamental inaccessibility of another man's psychic or subjective phenomena (as we may call them because of their being bound to a person or subject) are characteristic of these inner experiences. Only the man who tries to explain the actions of a fellow creature, be it a man or an animal, in terms of such subjective experience, may rightly call himself a psychologist. How far such an explanation of behaviour is possible, especially with the animals, is a question we shall soon have to consider.

This statement that psychology is the science of subjective phenomena will perhaps not satisfy the man who regards psychology as the science of the soul. Modern psychology, however, is a branch of the natural sciences, and in natural sciences there is no place for the concept of soul. Not that these sciences reject this concept, or doubt the reality of the soul, but they realize that it belongs to branches of knowledge, such as philosophy or metaphysics, that do not form part of natural science. The soul is an object of speculation, not of observation or experiment, and it is this difference in their method of approaching their object that separates natural sciences from the philosophic disciplines. Modern psychology, therefore, has rightly been called "a psychology without a soul." If animal psychology were to be the science of the animal soul, it would involve us in speculations about a survival of this soul after the death of the animal and the possibility of metempsychosis and so on. The scientific value of such a science would certainly be trifling.

The object of animal psychology, then, is not the animal soul but *the psychic phenomena in animals*. Its ultimate aim is to arrive at so complete a knowledge of these phenomena that it becomes possible to understand the psychical structure, be it of an animal or of a group of them, i.e. the dependence of one such phenomenon on the other, the gearing of one into the other, the remodelling of one by the other, in a way similar to that in which the anatomist or the physiologist tries to acquire a knowledge of the anatomical or physiological structure of the animal he is studying. That animal psychology is yet far from having reached this ideal is a fact we need scarcely mention.

But now the question arises whether an animal psychology conceived in this way is possible, or if it is an ideal that will never be realized, be it either because such phenomena do not occur in animals, or that they do occur but are not knowable to us.

Many people, indeed, doubt the possibility of a science of psychic phenomena in animals. Human psychology, they say, is built up on two foundations : the introspection into one's own inner experiences and the communication in human language of that which another man experiences at a given moment or under given conditions. It will be clear that both methods fail us when we try to study the animal mind. Introspection is of course directly precluded. And as to communication of inner experiences, it is very doubtful if an animal could ever be really explicitly conscious of what it experiences at a given moment, that it could realize for instance : "Now I am afraid, now I desire to kill that prey," which, of course, is quite another thing from the being afraid or the feeling of the desire itself. And even if, perhaps, some higher animal should arrive at a more or less vague realization of its inner feelings or desires, it is doubtful if it will ever feel any need to communicate them to other creatures. The animal, as a rule, is an egocentric being. If in fear it utters a particular cry, it may be that other members of its species, or perhaps even members of other species, will know this cry and may be affected by it in such a way that the feeling of fear of the one individual spreads through the whole troop. Yet there is no reason to admit that the first animal uttered its cry in order to communicate its feelings to the others. The uttering of the cry was nothing more than the expression, or the effect, of the feeling itself. Perhaps where there exists a strong social bond between two animals of the same species, as between child and mother, or even perhaps in rare cases where there is a social bond between an animal and man, as in the attachment of the dog to his master, there may be something like a need for communication of inner experience. But even then it might be asked if such inner feelings are clearly and explicitly experienced by the animal, and if this seeming need for communication is anything more than a clinging to a fellow creature at a moment of strong inner feeling or desire. Anyhow, these cases are so exceptional, and the communication itself is so vague, that they cannot suffice as bases on which to build a science.

For human psychology, to tell the truth, mere introspection into one's own inner experiences and the communication of such experiences by other people, are not sufficient as a basis for this science either. This is particularly the case when human psychology does not deal merely with the psychic life of the normal adult civilized man, as was too often the case formerly, but also with that of the young child, the primitive man, and the mentally diseased. Then the same difficulties arise as with the animals, though in a lesser degree. These persons, also, are not able scientifically to gauge their own inner experiences, nor are they able, or even willing, to communicate them clearly to others. Yet these branches of psychology flourish, and no one would think of denying their right of existence.

What, then, is the way these branches of human psychology overcome the difficulties arising from this lack or defectiveness of active assistance from the side of the objects of their study ? They do it by applying another method in which these objects play a more passive part, namely that of *observation and interpretation of their behaviour.* That is, we watch their actions while they believe themselves unobserved, we ask them questions of different kinds and note their answers, whether clear or vague, we bring them into unusual situations and watch how they help themselves out of them, etc. We observe all their expressions of emotion and feeling, be they spontaneous expressions or reactions to the situation we brought them into. And from the store of observations we collect in this way we draw conclusions as to their inner experience, their feeling, their thinking, their desiring.

Let us not overlook the fact that it is a great and relatively uncertain step we take when from objective observations of the behaviour of a man we draw conclusions as to the inner experiences that drive and guide him to his acts. For as we have seen, these inner experiences are known to us as existing in ourselves alone. That our fellow man has experiences of the same nature as we have, that he has kindred feelings and desires and sensations, is only a more or less probable supposition. A psychological solipsism, the attribution of such experiences to ourselves alone, is a logically defensible position, though doubtless nobody with a sane mind will adopt it. We are all sure that our fellow-man sees the light of the stars and feels the warmth of the sun just as we do, that our child is afraid in the dark or enjoys his play, that our adversary nurses a feeling of hatred or dislike to us and desires to thwart our plans. Nay, more, we know this to be sure knowledge. Why are we so sure about it ; how do we know it ? It has often been asserted that we know these inner experiences of our fellow men by way of analogy : if his movements or gestures were the same as we make in particular circumstances, we might therefore conclude that he is stirred by similar feelings as we experience when making the same gestures. This assumption, however, only partly holds true. In many cases we know what stirs a man, even if he does not make any movement or strike any attitude ; in many cases also we feel that a man is feigning and with a kind smile covers a feeling of hatred towards us. The young baby, on the other hand, when it sees its mother smiling kindly at it, knows the gentle feeling of the mother even if it has never had the opportunity to see itself laughing in a mirror, and responds to her gentle feeling by smiling back at her. The truth is that this understanding of other men occurs in quite a different way, that is, by a *sympathetic intuition*, the nature and the working of which it is not our task to discuss here. We may, perhaps, provisionally define this intuition as the faculty for directly grasping the essence of a reality, without preceding intellectual analysis. That this way of understanding may later on be supplemented and facilitated by a knowledge of the meaning of certain facial and other expressions in our fellow men that we have learned to distinguish by the experience of our own life, does not detract at all from the fact that originally our knowledge of other people's inner experiences is acquired in a different way.

If, now, we pass to the animals and the knowledge of their inner experiences, we are up against a similar, even though a greater, difficulty to that which we encounter when we study the psychology of the young child or primitive man. That the difficulty is greater nobody will deny, but fundamentally it is the same. It is greater because the mental difference between ourselves and the animals is far greater than that between ourselves and the child. But yet in principle it is the same : we make the great leap when we deduce from our inner experiences those of other people, and once granted the existence of psychic phenomena in other men and the possibility of our knowing them, the leap from them to the animals is not so formidable, especially if we believe that animal and man are cognate beings, originating from each other by way of evolution and forming a part of the same stream of life. When we admit psychic phenomena in other men, and believe we are more or less able to understand them, there is in principle no reason to deny them to animals or to think that we shall never be able to know them here also.

Since the difficulty in knowing the subjective experiences is the same in our fellow men and the animals, the method of overcoming this difficulty must also be similar in both cases. With the animals, therefore, our knowledge of their psychic life is also primarily based on sympathetic intuition. Let no one accuse us of unscientific phantasy or mysticism. Every one of us possesses this faculty and makes use of it in his everyday life. The man who whistles in vain for his dog and says : "He hears me very well, but he won't come, and tries to keep away from me, because he is afraid I will beat him," by way of sympathetic intuition has entered into the perceptions as well as into the feelings and the striving of his dog. And the man who warns a stranger to beware of a bull because he is vicious, shows the same kind of knowledge of the inner experiences of the bull as the man who makes a similar remark about a tribe of head-hunters in the jungle. Why, then, should such a knowledge suddenly cease, or fade away, when we pass from the field or the street into the lecture room or the laboratory ?

There is, however, a difference between an acknowledgment in principle and an acknowledgment in fact. The possibility that animals are mere automata without any inner life, as Descartes believed, or rather that the lower orders are such, as was contended by Loeb, cannot be ruled out by logical arguments alone, and intuition may deceive us. Empiricism must bring the solution, must support or invalidate our views. What, then, have the empirical facts to tell us about the reality of psychic phenomena in animals, quite apart from the question of their finer nature ?

We have seen already that the method of studying the inner experiences of animals is to watch their *behaviour*. We are using here the word "behaviour" in a somewhat restricted sense, given to it by McDougall, who connotes by this word all human or animal activity in which mental processes find expression. Hence the question now is whether the animals, it may be only some of them, show behaviour in this sense of the word.

How do we recognize behaviour, how do we know that the activity of animals is not merely the result of mechanical or physiological causation ? On this point William James has given us a useful hint. "The pursuance of future ends," he writes in the introduction of his *Principles of Psychology* "and the choice of means for their attainment, are the mark and criterion of the presence of mentality in a phenomenon." Where we find these facts we may conclude that inner experiences underlie the animals' activity, may infer the existence of real behaviour, therefore, in the McDougallian sense of the word.

These remarks of James, however, are rather vague, and it will not always be easy to apply them to observed animal activity. McDougall, therefore, has rendered us a great service in further elaborating this idea of James and in analysing his criterion into seven more profound *"marks of behaviour."* By reason of their supreme importance to us it seems worth while shortly to record them here.

The first of these marks that distinguish real behaviour, guided by inner experience, from the mechanical movements as we find in lifeless objects, is that of its *spontaneity*, i.e. the independence of the activity from external causation. The beginning of real behaviour is not determined by external forces working on the subject but by an inner state or inner experience in the subject itself. A stone remains lying still till some outer force sets it in motion ; when a man is sitting on a hill looking at the view before him, it is not external forces that drive him to move away but the consideration that it is time to go home or the fear of catching cold, or something similar. And when it is a threatening thunderstorm that impels him to move off and seek shelter he is not set in motion by the force of the wind or the darkness of the sky, but these perceptions inspire in him fear of getting wet, or confidence that the shower will pass over, and these inner feelings decide whether he goes or stays, and in the former case at what moment. Certainly, where there is such spontaneity in a phenomenon there is mentality in it.

The second mark of behaviour is that of the *persistence* of the action, independent of the continuation of what induced it. If the electric current that drives the train is interrupted, the train comes to a standstill. When the fear of the thunderstorm that induced the man to move has disappeared, he may continue his way home. And, then, there is a great difference between the motion of the stone rolling down hill when set in motion and that of the man running down hill in search of shelter. The former rolls down in an ever-increasing and computable velocity along a track that also may be indicated beforehand. The man may go more quickly or more slowly, as he likes, may make a detour around a block or rock or a pool of water, may choose this tree for a shelter or that, and may perhaps afterwards change his place for a better one. His action cannot be determined beforehand as was the movement of the stone. This brings us to a third mark of behaviour: that of the possible *variability* of its movements, that of the relative freedom of its action.

A fourth mark of behaviour is its *termination* as soon as the goal is reached. When the man has found a hut to take shelter in he does not go farther, even if the path goes on and he himself is not tired. The stone, on the other hand, rolls down hill till the valley is reached, or some obstacle prevents it going further. And a fifth mark is that of the *preparation* for, or anticipation of, a future activity. Before the man reaches his house he will take the key out of his pocket to open the door. That the rolling stone does not show any such preparations need not be emphasized.

We may summarize these five marks of behaviour as the mark of the independence of the action from outer forces, alike in its incipience, its progression and its completion. If any activity shows these five marks we do not doubt but that inner experience leads it, be it in a man or another creature.

McDougall has given two other marks of real behaviour which, however, are not so generally applicable to all cases where activity is observed. The first of these is that of its *increase in effectiveness* if the activity be repeated a second or third time under similar circumstances. If brought back to its former place, the stone does not on a second occasion roll

2

down more quickly or better than before, but if the man a second time has to take refuge at the same point, led by the experience of the former occasion he will sooner and more easily find a good shelter than the first time. This profiting by former experience cannot of course always be demonstrated and certainly not in the case where an animal or man executes an act for the first time in his life. Therefore this mark is not of such primary importance as the first five are, although the profiting by former experience itself is prominent in the behaviour of animals and is, as we shall see in a later chapter, the basis of what may be regarded as intelligent actions.

The seventh mark McDougall gave for the recognition of real behaviour is that of the *totality* of the action. Behaviour is a total reaction in which the whole individual is involved. This mark does not so much distinguish the behaviour of the man from the movement of the rolling stone, but does distinguish it from the working of a reflex. A few words on these reflexes, therefore, may not be superfluous, the more so as some confusion prevails on this point.

What, then, is a reflex? A reflex is a typical physiological phenomenon, wholly explicable by the laws of mechanical causation. When a physical stimulus strikes a sense-organ, or nerve-ends, this stimulus is propagated along a centripetal nerve-fibre to a centre, in which it is transmitted to a centrifugal fibre along which it is conducted to an organ, which hereby is roused to a characteristic activity, be it the contraction of a muscle or the secretion of a gland. Necessary for the functioning of a reflex, therefore, is a morphological structure, the so-called reflex-arc, consisting of at least five parts : the receptor in which the stimulus is received, the afferent nerve along which it is conducted to the centre, the centre itself as the place of transmission, the efferent nerve along which the stimulus is then carried to the effector, and the effector in which the stimulus provokes the movement. In many cases the reflexes are not so simple as described here : one reflex may induce a second and this a third, so that chains of reflexes may arise from the original stimulus ; also higher centres may interfere and influence the effect of the phenomenon. This, however, does not essentially change the nature of the reflex-process. Characteristic of a reflex are thus the morphological structure that underlies the propagation of the stimulus and the mechanical course of the whole process.[1]

Now it must be said here that many persons often use the word reflex in a much wider sense so that it completely loses its original meaning and means nothing more than a reaction to a stimulus, however complicated these two may be, whatever be their nature, and however many factors may be involved in them. If an animal sees and recognizes an enemy and flies in fear, then this is called a "flight-reflex." When one of Pavlov's dogs tried to liberate himself from an apparatus in which he had been shut up for an experiment, Pavlov attributed this action to a "liberation-reflex" of the dog, and when another dog showed interest in some changes in the experiment-room this was attributed to a "what-is-that-reflex"! It will be clear that such a watering down and so slovenly a use of scientific terms cannot be sufficiently condemned. The fault in doing so is that first one emphasizes a special characteristic of a term in the original restricted sense (e.g. its mechanical causation), then applies the term to a number of phenomena that were not originally comprised in the definition, and then endeavours to suggest that "therefore" all these phenomena show the characteristics that belong solely to the phenomena that answer to the original definition. To avoid such errors it is necessary to keep to the original meaning of the word reflex, and to speak of a reflex only when a real reflex-arc is, or at least can be theoretically, shown.

If, then, we ask ourselves what is the principal difference between a reflex and a real action, we feel that this difference lies in the nature of the experience that attends both. When

---

[1] *Has the reflex reality?* Some physiologists (Bethe, Buytendyk) doubt it. In their opinion a real isolated reflex does not occur. The reflex, then, is only an abstraction made by the human mind, the reflex-arc only a hypothetical construction. The splitting up of a function into reflexes is artificial, as is the division of a body into organs, and of its activity into functions. In reality, they all form one cohering unity. It will be clear, however, that for us this question is of but secondary importance ; for the interpretation of animal activity the difference between a real or ideal reflex and an action remains the same.

executing a reflex movement we feel ourselves as passive ;
when carrying out an action we feel ourselves as active. When
by a blow on or below the knee-cap our shin and foot are
suddenly thrown up in the well-known knee-jerk, we experience this movement as something that is done to us, not as
something that we do ourselves. We have an entirely different
experience if when sitting on a bench in the park we make a
similar movement to chase a dog away. And when we cough
because something tickles our throat we have a different
experience than when we do it to draw the attention
of a person who is walking before us in the street.
Many reflexes, like the pupillary reflex, or the secretion of
the gastric glands, even occur below the threshold of our
consciousness.

Now with animals this distinction mostly fails us. We do
not as a rule know the inner experiences of a certain animal
at a particular moment sufficiently to know for certain
whether some movement it produces is undergone passively
by it or is the result of an active striving. In such cases
McDougall's seventh mark may be a great help. The reflex,
then, is a partial reaction, a reaction of a limited part of the
body to a simple stimulus ; in an act, in real behaviour, the
whole animal is involved. Real behaviour, therefore, can be
found only there where the unity of the organism has not
been broken ; reflexes may be shown even by isolated parts
of the body. If the head of an insect has been severed from
the body, biting reflexes may be provoked, but only the intact
animal really bites. A decapitated grasshopper may show the
jumping reflex, but it does not spread out its wings in doing
so, as does the normal animal when taking a flying leap.
The decapitated copperhead-snake may strike when its tail
is pinched and may even strike in the direction of the pinch,
but according to Huxley there is a great difference between
the blind and automatic striking of this part of the animal
and the action of attacking, which is guided by perceptions
and may be inhibited by fear or other vital interests of the
animal as a whole.

Where, therefore, we see an animal acting as an organic
whole, we may regard this as a proof of real behaviour, and

need not consider this activity as the outcome of one or more reflexes. It will be clear that this knowledge gives us a weapon in our hands against the physiologist if he tries to divert us from the interpretation of the activity of some animal by proclaiming that this is nothing but the result of the working of some reflexes.

But let us return to the seven marks of McDougall. Wherever we find in the activity of an animal these marks of spontaneity, of variation, of termination, of persistence, of preparation, of improvement, where we see the animal acting as a whole, we may be sure this activity is not governed by external mechanical causation, but is evoked by inner experiences, being an expression of perceptions and feelings, of desires and drives. Where we find them, we find real behaviour, and at the same time we find in the animal a serviceable object for our study of animal psychology.

Let us now test some animals and see if they can be used to this end.

For the higher animals this examination is not difficult, nor the issue of it uncertain. Let us take the case of a dog lying quietly in the room while his master is reading. Suddenly, and without any perceptible reason, the dog rises and goes to his master. His course through the room is unpredictable : he may go round the right side of the table or round the left side, he may go slowly, or quickly, and certainly his going will differ one evening from that of the day before. When he reaches his master he sits down and looks at him in expectation. If the master gives some sign, if, for instance, he rises from his chair, the dog runs to the door and stands there waiting till the master opens the door to let him out. If this happens several times the dog will show an improvement in his behaviour, in so far as he does not wait till his master has risen, but runs to the door as soon as his master looks inquiringly at him, as he has learnt by experience that this look is a preliminary to his master's rising from his chair. Doubtless the behaviour of the dog is accompanied and guided by inner experiences, as weariness, impatience, desire, expectance, joy, in some cases disappointment and sadness, which, in the case of the dog, may easily be read from his attitude and sounds, the movements of his body and tail, the look in his eyes, etc.

Instead of a dog we might have chosen a monkey, a bird, a snake, a fish. Everywhere in these groups we should have found unmistakable proofs of behaviour, guided by inner experiences. It is not necessary to quote examples. One has merely to watch the behaviour of some voracious fish, say a pike or a perch in a stream or aquarium, to find here the marks of spontaneity, of variability, of persistence and so on. That fishes may learn, that is, may profit by good or bad experience, is a fact every angler knows and that is surely known also to the student of sense physiology, who realizes that the experiments on colour vision, form discrimination, hearing and so on in fishes, are all founded on the method of training, i.e. of the modification of innate reactions in the light of past experience.

Let us now pass to another class of animals, the insects : ants, bees, wasps, and the like. At the very beginning of this chapter our curiosity was aroused by the spontaneity of the ant returning on her path without any perceptible external reason, and the same characteristics may be observed in the bee flying round a heather bush in search of food. Solitary wasps dig a hole in the ground, and there endeavour to collect a store of caterpillars or spiders as food for their future offspring. The Peckhams, who closely studied the behaviour of these animals, lay stress on the great variability in their behaviour in their striving to attain this end, and even go so far as to term this variability the "one prominent, unmistakable and ever-present fact" in this behaviour. This holds true for the conduct of different individuals of the same species as well as for the successive actions of one individual. The making of the hole itself may be regarded as a preparation for the future storing of provision. In her search for a caterpillar, or a spider, the hunting wasp persistently goes on exploring the territory round her nest till a prey has been discovered ; then she stops flying about and proceeds with a different action. That insects may learn by experience to change or improve upon innate actions is again shown by the ease with which bees can be trained to react to special colours or forms, if these prove to indicate a source of food, and from the fact that they easily and readily come back to a place where once food has been found, be it a field of flowering heather in the case of the bee, or, in the case of the wasp, the table of a family taking tea in the open air.

It will be clear that the same must be true of the larvae of insects. From a psychological point of view there is of course no reason to make a distinction between the larva and the perfect insect. The insect is a living, perceiving and striving being before as well as after metamorphosis, however great the morphological differences between the two stages of life may be. Caterpillars, caddis flies, larvae of beetles and suchlike show the same characteristics in their behaviour that we found sufficient in other animals for the assumption of psychic phenomena. Let us show this by one example, which some time ago acquired some notoriety as an instance of the contrary.

The ant-lion, larva of the Neuropteron Myrmeleo, passes its larval life at the bottom of a funnel-like pit, built by itself in the sand. If ants, or other small insects, happen to get into this pit they slide down, together with the sand of the walls of the pit, and fall into the open mandibles of the larva, which seizes them and pulls them under the sand, where it kills them and sucks them out. If by chance an ant succeeds in freeing itself from the ant-lion's mandibles and tries to climb the walls of the pit, the ant-lion throws up the sand that the ant in its flight sends down. In most cases this hits the fugitive ant and causes it to slip down again.

Now, some thirty years ago Doflein alleged that the whole behaviour of the ant-lion could be explained by assuming three simple mechanical reflexes : a digging-reflex, causing the larva to disappear under the sand, a throwing-reflex, which makes it throw up the sand in digging its pit and in pursuit of the flying ant, and a snapping-reflex, causing the mandibles to close whenever an insect is between them. He herewith declared the ant-lion to be a reflex-automaton, a machine without any trace of psychical life, thereby returning to the view which Descartes had defended long before him regarding the whole animal kingdom. That the term reflex was not very felicitous will be clear : when the animal disappears under the ground there is more involved in this action than a local reaction of some part of the body, and clearly the animal as a whole is working to some end. But the essential question is : Is the entire activity of the animal mechanically determined by some few external stimuli ? Later observers of the ant-lion's behaviour came to quite a different result. They found spontaneity in the behaviour of the animal, especially when, without any outer stimulus, it suddenly began to dig a new canal in the sand, probably stirred by some feeling of uneasiness as a result of non-optimal conditions of the surroundings. A similar spontaneity might sometimes be observed when, after the prey was taken away from him by the experimenter, the animal suddenly started to throw up sand, although in this case it had not been struck by sand thrown down by the escaping prey. It was even observed that the ant-lion in the pursuit of a fugitive ant went so far as to turn round in its pit, and even now and then to leave it. In the act of catching its prey a great variability could be observed. Thus a wildly struggling ant is sometimes caught and stunned by being beaten against the walls of the pit ; an ant that is not rightly caught is thrown up and caught better when it comes down again. In the position the ant-lion takes at the bottom of its pit, with the mandibles open to catch any falling victim, we may see the preparation for a coming act. Even an ant-lion showed itself capable of learning by experience : it could be trained to accept and eat dead flies instead of living ants. And when the author put an ant-lion and an ant together in a glass tube and let them fight together there, he observed in the larva as well as in the ant a purposive activity with sudden outbursts of spontaneity, a persistence in the action when stimulation from the side of the enemy was wanting, and an effective variation in the action itself, such as a machine or an automaton would never show.

It will be clear that Doflein's judgment of the character of the ant-lion was only the result of a too superficial and biassed observation. The source of his error may be partially found in the fact that the ant-lion is a highly specialized creature, living in simple natural surroundings with simple and almost unvarying characteristics. In such surroundings the actions of an animal are often inclined to become simplified to a few uniform and seemingly automatic movements, and thus, on a superficial observer, may make the impression of being no more than reflexes. Some simple experiments, however, suffice to demonstrate their real nature. If the ant-lion is taken from its pit and brought into another environment, for instance into a small box covered with a glass plate, its behaviour at once loses much of the stereotypy it evinced in the sand, and certainly no longer makes the impression of being of a reflex character.

It is not necessary to pass through all classes of the animal kingdom in search of marks of real behaviour, of proofs of psychic phenomena. Let us rather pass on directly to the Protozoa. Is real behaviour, bearing the marks of psychic life, observable in these creatures ? The importance of this question will be clear. If real psychic life be found here, where we stand at the roots of animal life, it will certainly be difficult to deny it in other animals.

If, then, we ask what observers of Protozoan life have found with regard to McDougall's criteria in the activity of these animals, thereby entitling us to assume psychic life and inner experiences in them, we must first of all rid ourselves of the prejudice that the small size of these animals would make it improbable, or even impossible, that their activity be governed by psychic experiences. It will be clear that there is no reason at all to believe that these immaterial phenomena are limited to a certain minimum size of the individual exhibiting them or that psychic life in this world correlates with the visual acuity of the human eye. Only a close observation of their activity and a critical interpretation of it can answer this question.

Now, first of all, many students of Protozoa have been struck by the spontaneity in their behaviour. Even so relatively early a writer as Verworn has pointed out the frequent occurrence in them of spontaneous movements, as contrasted with movements caused by external stimuli. As instances of these spontaneous movements he mentioned the swimming movements and especially the abrupt changes in the direction and velocity of the swimming in Bacteria and Flagellata, the seeking movements of the flagellum of Euglena and kindred forms, the movements of the pseudopodia of Amoeba, the sudden contractions of stalked Infusoria, like Stentor and Vorticella, for which he could never find any external stimulus, etc. Especially striking are the spontaneous movements of Infusoria which, like Halteria, possess spring-cilia and first swim forwards with the help of their adoral cilia, then suddenly, without any perceivable reason, turn back and swim on in another direction. In Amoeba, Jennings described a remarkable spontaneous action : if Amoeba has been suspended for some time in the water without contact with any fixed object, it stretches out long pseudopodia to all sides and searches the surroundings till one of the pseudopodia comes into contact with a solid object. Then the tip of that pseudopodium attaches itself to the object, and the animal, while drawing in the other pseudopodia, gets on to it. Here we have an instance, not only of spontaneity of behaviour on the part of the Protozoan, but also one of persistence in the action till the end, viz. contact with a fixed body, has been attained, and of the termination of the act of seeking as soon as this is accomplished. Certainly we cannot find the motive for the seeking action in any external stimulus; it is, on the contrary, the lack of all external stimulation that induces the activity of Amoeba.

But here perhaps the physiologist who has so far silently, although more or less reluctantly, followed the line of our argumentation, will stop and interrupt us. As long as it was only a question of higher animals, say of dogs, or fishes, or even insects, he could acquiesce in the idea that inner experiences played a part in their behaviour. But with unicellular being, "a speck of protoplasm with a nucleus," as he has learned to call them, this goes too far for him. He is willing to grant that no external forces led Amoeba to its search. But does this prove that psychic processes underlie this activity ? Is it not possible to ascribe the searching for a fixed object by Amoeba to some physiological state in the animal, say some tiredness, that impels it to seek a resting place ? Or, to put the question on a higher plane, is the mark of spontaneity, and are the marks of McDougall in general, really sufficient to prove psychic phenomena in animals ? Is there not another possibility for the explanation of their behaviour when external mechanical causation is ruled out, viz., the working of purely physiological inner processes ?

In answer to this we may say we are willing to assume some form of "tiredness" as the origin of the action described of Amoeba. But, then, is such a "tiredness" of purely physiological, i.e. physico-chemical, nature ? Let us guard against the old confusion between physiology and psychology, between physiological and psychological phenomena ! A purely physico-chemical state of tiredness will never lead to anything else than inactivity in an animal, and only if it be accompanied by some feeling of uneasiness, discomfort, or such like, however vague and diffuse these feelings may be, will this feeling of tiredness induce a spontaneous and, in its details unpredictable, behaviour like that of Amoeba, when seeking for some fixed point with outstretched pseudopodia. More generally speaking : a purely physiological, i.e. physico-chemical state or a physico-chemical phenomenon in a living being, not accompanied by any psychical concomitant, may have as a result some physico-chemical process in the body of the animal, and may even perhaps in Amoeba be the cause of an expulsion of protoplasma in the form of pseudopodia. It is unconceivable, however, that such a physico-chemical state, or an integration of physico-chemical processes alone, may induce an animal to purposive directive striving, exhibiting characteristics belonging to an essentially different domain from that of physico-chemical reactions and physico-chemical causality. Wherever we find a spontaneous, persistent, variable, directive behaviour of an animal as a whole, be it in a dog or in an Amoeba, we come no further with an explanation by inner physiological processes than with an explanation by outer mechanical causation.

It will further be clear that an appeal to the concept of reflex offers no help to the physiologist in this dilemma.

In the first place, as far as the Protozoa are concerned, it is questionable if real reflexes occur in them. Jennings, at least, doubts this. But even if we confine ourselves to the higher animals, where reflexes certainly are to be found, they cannot explain real behaviour. We have already seen that the reflex, if this concept is to have any meaning at all, comprises partial mechanical reactions to physico-chemical stimulations. Such reflexes, then, may be integrated to complex wholes, but do not thereby change their real nature. Reflexes, or integrations of reflexes, may show a passive mechanical purposefulness, as the purposefulness of a typewriter or an atomic bomb ; they never show the directiveness, the active purposiveness, the "pursuance of future ends" of behaviour. The purposive can never be explained by the mechanical, nor can real behaviour ever be wholly analysed into reflexes.

But let us return to the Protozoa to see if they show more marks of real behaviour.

The best occasion to observe such behaviour with all its characteristic signs is to be found when an animal shows the highest tension of its vitality, that is, when retreating from an advancing enemy, or when itself hunting a prey. This hunting by the Protozoa has several times been observed and reported on by various authors. Engelmann described such chasing by a Voticella, that followed a smaller one for some time but was unable to catch it, and finally lost it when the smaller one made a sudden turn. Binet described the hunting by Ciliates as a real chase, in which perception and localization of the prey and purposive activity, played a rôle. The most elaborate description of the chasing by Amoeba we find in Jennings. He describes the pursuit by an Amoeba of a round cyst of Euglena, and, more interesting yet, the chase by an Amoeba of a smaller one, that not merely rolled passively away as did the cyst, but actually tried to escape from the pursuer. It would take too long to quote here Jennings' description in full ; for the details we must refer to Jennings' own account. It may suffice here to state that, according to this writer, Amoeba behaves in a way similar to that which would be adopted by some higher animal in the same case, the entire hunting being one coherent process in which the whole animal is involved. A dissolution into a number of simple reactions to stimuli is, according to Jennings, difficult, or even impossible ; a variation of the means employed, a persistence till the end is reached and a termination of the action when this has taken place, are the most striking characteristics in this behaviour.

The imbibing of food by Amoeba is also a more complex activity than was formerly believed. That it cannot simply be explained by changes in the tension of the surface layer alone, as has sometimes been asserted, that on the contrary it requires actual activity on the part of the Amoeba, has been shown by Mast and Root, and by Beers. More important, however, is the great variability in the behaviour while capturing the prey, as has been shown by Kepner and his fellow workers. An immobile prey is closely embraced by the protoplasma of the Amoeba ; to a mobile prey the flight is first blocked in a wider embrace, then the prey is embraced more closely in different ways depending on the behaviour of the prey itself. Amoeba may form one or more secondary pseudopods of different sizes, it may withdraw its pseudopods at unsuitable places while it may form new ones more suitable, etc. According to Kepner, all these reactions are entirely independent of the stimulation of Amoeba by its prey ; they may be stopped or reversed, should that be required by the aim Amoeba is striving for by ever-varying means.

We therefore find in Protozoa the same marks of behaviour that we know in higher organisms : spontaneity, variation in the means employed, persistence of action and cessation of it when the end has been reached, independently of the momentary working of the stimulus. That Amoeba reacts as an organized whole has been especially stressed by Mast. And even some years ago it was shown by Bramstedt that Protozoa may learn to profit by experience.

This was demonstrated in the following way. Bramstedt put some Paramaecia into a drop of water in which a temperature gradient of 15° was produced. The warm half of the drop was then illuminated, while the cold one was kept dark. Now, if the animals swimming in the drop happened to get into the warm half of it, they showed their well-known

evading reaction, and returned to the cold part. Then after
1—1½ hours both parts of the drop were equally heated.
Although there was now no external reason why the animals
should avoid the lighter half of the drop, they yet remained
in the dark part and exhibited evasive reactions when cross-
ing the boundary between the dark and light, which reactions
were not shown by animals that had not been trained before.
They had therefore learned by experience to associate light
with heat. This experience was only retained for some 15
minutes, after which the effects of training were lost, probably
by the new experience that light now no more meant heat.
With a creeping Infusorium, Bramstedt succeeded in a
similar way in forming an association between light and a
rough surface, between darkness and a smooth one. Bramstedt's results have later been confirmed by Soest, and
extended by the latter to other Protozoa.

From all these facts we may draw the conclusion that the
behaviour of Protozoa shows the marks we had previously
recognized as proofs of psychic phenomena underlying the
activity of a living being. We may therefore credit the Protozoa
with experiences such as sensations and feelings, desires and
drives, of the same nature, though undoubtedly vaguer and
more diffuse, than those we know in ourselves. It will be
clear that this conclusion is highly important. For if we admit
an inner psychic life in Protozoa, we cannot deny it to other
animals. It is very improbable, to say the least of it, that
psychic phenomena occurring in Protozoa are lacking in
higher animals that have descended from similar b eings in
the course of the evolution of animal life. The difference
between a perceiving, feeling and striving being and a finely
constructed machine is too fundamental to make such a
supposition admissible. This of course does not imply that
everywhere in the animal world psychic life can be demonstrated with such relative ease as in Protozoa (especially in
Amoeba and similar active species). In sessile animals, like
the Coelenterata, the Ascidia and the Bryozoa, it will be
difficult to prove real behaviour. Their sessile life give them
little opportunity to show a purposive striving. In them we
observe little of any spontaneity of behaviour, of a variation

in the means, of a persistence and a preparation, and of a profiting by experience. In their way of living they show great resemblance to plants, regarding which Aristotle said that they were "animals fallen asleep."

Yet most of them, during their larval life, pass through a stadium of free movement, and in this stage show the same kind of behaviour as do free-living plankton organisms. Larvae of Ascidia at the beginning of their life are negatively geotactic and strive to reach the surface of the water ; later they become positively geotactic and make for the bottom of the sea, where they attach themselves in preparation to their metamorphosis. It is of course incredible that all psychic life should wholly disappear with their transition to their final phase. And even such sessile animals from time to time show marks of real behaviour. Spontaneous activity may be observed in Hydra which, if it has been left undisturbed for a long time, may suddenly leave its place and move about until finally it fixes itself at another place, probably having been stirred by some feeling of uneasiness or discomfort. Loeb found that if the Actinia Cerianthus is put upside down into a test tube, the animal in directive action wriggles to get back into its normal position. In the origin of the symbiosis between an anemone and a crab the active part is not always played by the crab ; in many cases the initiative emanates from the Actinia that strives to get on the back of a crab and in this sometimes shows a distinct preparation for the act of climbing on to the crab's back even before a crab is anywhere in the neighbourhood.

These few examples may suffice to show that in sessile animals psychic life is not always so dormant that it could not be recognized in their activity. This justifies the recognition of psychic phenomena in all animals. Of course such an admission does not say anything further about the nature of these phenomena ; in particular it says nothing about the degree of consciousness that accompanies and illuminates it. In ourselves we know all gradations of clearness of consciousness of our inner experiences, from those which occur wholly, or nearly, subconsciously to those that take place in the clearest light of our apperceptive attention. We will do well

to admit that, especially with the lower animals, psychic
phenomena will for the most part take place in the twilight
of a half-conscious state, illuminated only from time to time
by flashes of a clearer consciousness.

We now know that we may admit psychic life in all
animals, that the whole animal kingdom belongs to the field
of study of the student of animal psychology. We know, too,
that in principle these psychic phenomena in animals are
knowable to us, in the same way as those of our fellow men.
We might expect, therefore, that all students of animal
behaviour would follow us and try to deduce from the
observed behaviour the psychic phenomena of which this
behaviour is the expression. But it is just here that we meet
with unwillingness on the part of the objectivists.

The *objectivist* is the man who (in most cases) does not
deny psychic life in animals as Descartes did, but does not
take pains to know it, pretending either that he has no
interest in it, or that he believes the knowledge he can obtain
of it to be too uncertain. He, therefore, voluntarily renounces
a knowledge he might be able to obtain. He studies animal
behaviour for its own sake, and is not willing to go farther
than the objectively knowable facts, and therefore remains
quite at the fringe of this behaviour, describing the acts of
the animals, asking what stimuli evoke these acts, but omitting
to consider what links an external stimulus to an external
reaction. In Germany there first arose such an objectivistic
movement when, at the end of the last century, three biologists, Beer, Bethe and von Uexküll, in a comprehensible
reaction to the rather uncritical animal psychology of those
days, published a manifesto in which they tried to clear the
sense physiology of men and animals from all expressions
that were contaminated with a subjective meaning, since, in
their opinion, subjective phenomena were only knowable in
ourselves, whereas in our fellow men, not to speak of animals,
they were knowable only by analogy. They therefore proposed
to speak of "receptors" instead of sense organs, of "recep-
tions" instead of sensations, of "icono-receptions" instead of
perceptions, and the like. Characteristic of their attitude was

von Uexküll's pronouncement : "We renounce deducing from observable action of the animals psychical phenomena in them." These phenomena, therefore, are not denied, but only ignored. From this standpoint von Uexküll later built up his "Umweltlehre," an interesting objective doctrine of animal behaviour, but one the further consideration of which would here be out of place.

The influence of this German objectivistic trend has never been very great. Most of the adherents turned to pure physiology. More influential was an American tendency to objectivism, the "Behaviourism," first expounded by Watson in a manifesto of 1913. There are among these Behaviourists many different tendencies and gradations, from the mechanistic and somewhat simplistic behaviourism of Watson himself to the "purposive Behaviourism" of Tolman, who oscillates between the Behaviourism of Watson on the one end and the Purposivism of McDougall on the other, and the "hormic Behaviourism" of Russell, who, although openly recognizing the animal as a feeling, perceiving, and striving subject, yet focusses attention not so much on these subjective phenomena themselves, but on the biological significance of the behaviour and its relation to other bodily activities. But they all agree on the one fact of acknowledging as the object of science only what is objectively knowable. In his later books Watson goes farther, and not only ignores subjective phenomena but even more or less denies them. Such concepts as sensation, sentiment, drive, memory, and the like, according to him, are scientifically worthless, and must be left to philosophy.

It cannot be denied that from a theoretical point of view such an objectivism is quite in its right. A man of science need not interest himself in every subject on earth and has the right to restrict the scope of his work : a student of history need not learn the languages of all the peoples whose past he studies, nor is it absolutely necessary for the student of comparative anatomy to study the distribution on the earth of the animals he uses in his comparisons. On the other hand it must be stated that in this case the objectivist remains much in default. If one is interested in describing and explaining the behaviour of animals, why stop at the description of objectively observable phenomena and not at least try to penetrate into the inner experiences of an animal that undoubtedly influence its behaviour ? Why speak only of a stimulus when we know that the animal reacts to what for it is more than a stimulus, namely : a perception ? Why ignore the feelings and strivings of the animal or at the best summarize them as "unknown internal factors" ? In the case of man surely nobody can be content with such a defective explanation. If an observer were to explain the behaviour of a man who tries to reach the shore after having fallen into the water simply as a complex movement of arms and legs, released by the stimulus of the humidity of the water, we should call this a very unsatisfactory interpretation of the facts observed. We should feel that in this description highly important and fundamental elements had been overlooked, such as the image in the man's mind of the expanse of deep water he is floating in, his fear of being drowned, his looking out for a place of safety and his actual striving to reach the shore, and we should know that all these inner experiences have influenced and governed his actions much more than the mere stimulation by contact with the water would do. In the same way if an objectivist (Tinbergen) believes to have sufficiently analysed the behaviour of a herring-gull settling on her eggs by saying that the visual stimulus of the eggs releases the innate movement of sitting down, we know that he overlooks the fact that in reality the chain has more links : the gull perceives the eggs, recognizes them as objects to be hatched, experiences some tender feeling towards those round objects, desires and strives to sit on them and, as a result of all this, executes the act of settling. If, by some cerebral lesion or mental disease, the gull should be struck by "psychic blindness" and should no longer recognize those round white objects that she sees as eggs, she probably would not settle on them, although the visual stimulus would remain the same. The whole chain, therefore, is built up in this way : visual stimulus—perception—feeling—drive—action, from which the three middle, psychic, factors of course cannot be omitted if a complete analysis is desired.

For the rest the attitude of many of the objectivists is curiously inconsistent. They claim to restrict themselves to the objective facts alone, but as they often feel the impossibility of really describing in this way what happens, they often supplement their description by using terms which have a psychological meaning, like "drive" or "mood," or the like, excusing themselves by saying that they use these terms "in an objective or physiological sense only." What a word like "mood," which describes a certain complex of feelings or emotional states, means in a physiological sense is not quite clear ; for the rest, the insertion of such subjective terms into an objective description is of course apt to cause confusion. This declaration of objectivism when using subjective terms is evidently done to quiet the objectivistic conscience of the writers concerned. Sometimes also they honestly own up to the insufficiency of their theoretical attitude when they say, like Nissen and Crawford in connection with the use of words like "unhappiness," "friendship," "sympathy" and such-like in their interesting description of the behaviour of chimpanzees : "We shall conserve time and space by employing anthropomorphic terms (without quotation marks) when these permit briefer or more adequate description than would available objective terminology." We may doubt if ever any really objective terminology will permit of an adequate description in this case.

Among these objectivists we may again distinguish two main trends. Some are content with the tracing of the stimulation that provokes a reaction, and the description of this reaction to the stimulus. Others go farther, and regard as their ultimate aim the analysis of the behaviour of the animals into the muscle contractions that are involved in it, or even, like Fraenkel and Gunn, into fundamental terms of physics and chemistry. Practically speaking there is no great difference between the latter and the physiologists we mentioned before, and with them we may speak of a "flight into physiology" for fear of acknowledging psychical phenomena in animals. It is clear that where the behaviour of an animal is thus split up into these ultimate elements, the animal as a whole is disregarded. For this reason we would give the preference to the former trend, if we had to choose between them.

But it is not our intention to depreciate the objectivists. They have done, and are still doing, excellent work in their careful descriptions of animal behaviour. Our task is to draw conclusions as to the inner factors in behaviour. Objectivistic study of the behaviour is the first step to be taken. But it is not necessary to limit ourselves to this first step. We may and must go farther.

Let us end this chapter now by summarizing our conclusions as to these fundamental problems of animal psychology. The object of animal psychology, then, is not the animal soul, a conception we readily leave to other sciences to speculate on ; it is to be found, rather, in the subjective or psychical phenomena of animals. Such phenomena we know directly in ourselves as our inner experiences of perceiving and feeling, of desiring and striving, of remembering and understanding and the like. In other creatures, in our fellow-men as well as in the animals, we know them only in an indirect way, namely, either with the aid of that other creature himself, who communicates to us what he experiences at a given moment, or without his aid, by studying and interpreting his behaviour. In animals we are confined to the latter way of study. The interpretation of their behaviour then is mainly based on a sympathetic intuition anent the animal's inner experiences, a faculty every man possesses to a certain degree and of which he makes use in his everyday life. Errors, of course, may be made, as regards the feelings and drives of the animal as well as the feelings and desires of the man, but in principle those inner experiences of animals are certainly knowable to us. And in applying to the animals the seven marks McDougall has brought to the fore for the recognition of real behaviour, i.e. activity provoked by inner experiences, we found such behaviour everywhere in the animal world, from the higher orders down to the Protozoa, so that we are entitled to include all animals in our psychological studies. For these two reasons there is no ground for us to share the objectivist's scepticism : we may commit ourselves to a genuine and frank animal psychology.

It will now be our task in the following pages to summarize in a few chapters the results of many years of study of this animal psychology.

CHAPTER II

THE PROBLEM OF ANIMAL INSTINCT

For, where there is sensation, there is also pleasure and pain and, where these, necessarily also desire.
Aristotle, *De Anima.* (Translation J. A. Smith.)

EVERY science which is more than a simple agglomeration of assumed facts, but which tries to build up a logical construction of theories and hypotheses that bind such facts together, has generally one or more central problems to which all these theories and hypotheses are related. For animal psychology this central problem is that of animal instinct.

What, then, is an instinct?

In the philosophy of the man in the street the view may often be heard that the animal is impelled to its acts by "instinct," man on the contrary by "intelligence." According to this way of thinking, instinct comprises all the psychical faculties of the animal ; it is, perhaps, even the only psychical quality with which the animal is credited. It is supposed to be some general, never-failing, mysterious, innate knowledge, which tells the animal in every circumstance of its life what it has to do and what it must avoid. Intelligence, on the other hand, a prerogative of man, is not such a "savoir faire inné" (Spaier), but a mental faculty which enables man consciously to choose the right means to attain some end, and to act after ample deliberation about the pros and cons of the performance of some act in a special circumstance.

This view, however, is certainly no more than a very crude approximation to the truth. That in the behaviour of animals instinct stands out more clearly than in that of man, that on the other hand the acts of man in many cases are executed after deliberation and are guided by the result of reflection, cannot be denied. But we know that in man also instinct, though it may be unnoticed by himself, often determines his actions. And that in the behaviour of animals intelligence may also play a part will be made clear in the course of this book. This old antithesis between instinct, as being alone responsible for the acts of animals, and intelligence, as being responsible for those of man, certainly cannot be maintained.

This antithesis, it must be admitted, is a very old one. Already the ancient Greeks, especially the Stoic philosophers, assumed in the animals as the springs of their actions a faculty of mind they called the *"Hormé"* (i.e. that which impels), and Scholasticism translated this word by *"instinctus"* from the Latin *"instinguere,"* which also means instigating, or impelling. And although both philosophies were more or less subject to the same fault we criticized just now in the popular psychology of the man in the street, the derivation of both terms from verbs that mean something like "incitation" or "impelling" shows that they consciously gave to the word instinct a psychological meaning. We will hold to this psychological meaning of the word.

It cannot be our intention to give a review of the great number of descriptions and definitions given in the course of time of this concept of instinct. Many of these satisfy us no longer, either because they give to the notion of instinct too wide a scope, whereby it comprises many phenomena that are better not included in it, or, on the other hand, they restrict it so much that even its psychological core sometimes gets lost. One of the best provisional definitions probably is that given by Romanes in his article on instinct in the ninth edition of the *Encyclopaedia Britannica* which runs as follows: "Instinct is a generic term comprising all those faculties of mind which lead to the (conscious) performance of actions that are adaptive in character but pursued without necessary knowledge of the relation between the means employed and the ends attained." We have put the word "conscious" between brackets because, as we saw in the first chapter, the degree of consciousness with which the animal performs an action is something we do not know about. For the rest, the word is not of primary importance in this definition.

Instinct, then, according to this definition is a psychological factor, comprising a number of "faculties of mind," i.e. of psychical phenomena, of inner experiences. What is the nature of these psychical phenomena, what is the relation between them, are questions we shall have to consider in this chapter. Instinct, or rather, instincts (for we have learned to give up here the idea of one simple general psychological faculty, and have come to distinguish between several instincts in the plural)—instincts, then, lead the animal to perform adaptive actions. Let us call these actions "instinctive actions," and distinguish them clearly from the instinct itself that calls them up, a distinction that is not always kept in view. These actions, then, are performed without the animal understanding their meaning and purpose : it does not know their "why" and "for what." The animal, acting on the urge of an instinct, mostly acts as if driven by a blind impulse. We may add yet two other characteristics of instincts, not mentioned by Romanes in his definition : they are innate and not acquired during the life of the animal, and they are characteristic for the whole species to which the animal belongs, not only for the individual animal. Let us illustrate all this by some examples from animal life.

Instincts and instinctive actions are characteristic of the species to which the animal belongs. All members of a species, or of a wider systematic group of animals, in similar circumstances behave in a similar instinctive way. At the end of the summer all our storks migrate to the South, and it does not depend on the individual decision of any one among them if he will depart or stay in the country. On the other hand, no house-sparrow undertakes such a journey but all remain in our country in winter. All spiders of the family of Agelenidae spin an irregular web of fine texture, and no one of them ever comes so far as to spin a regular orb-web which we all know as a characteristic of the family of Epeiridae. Among the birds the family of the Columbidae, according to Lorenz, is distinguished from other families of birds by no common morphological characteristic, but they distinguish themselves from other birds by their drinking instinct, the act of which consists in a rhythmical sucking up of the water with submerged beak, while the other birds drink by putting their bill into the water and then raising their head. Spaier even goes so far as to distinguish animals in general from plants as organisms subject to the working of instincts.

Instincts and instinctive actions in this way become characteristics of a species, just like the morphological ones on which as a rule the distinction between the species of animals is founded. The same holds true for the results of instinctive actions. By the nest of a bird we may recognize the species of the animal that built it, just as we may recognize this by the colour of its feathers. The insects stored in the nest of a digger-wasp tell us the species of the wasp that buried them, just like the colour of the abdomen or the form of the antennae of the wasps themselves. In some cases the instinctive actions of animals may give even better and clearer marks of distinction than do morphological ones. We have seen this already for the family of pigeons. According to Wachs the courtship of sea-birds shows characteristic differences that are much more important than the morphological differences generally used to characterize the different species. The common and the Arctic tern (Sterna hirundo and paradisea) show but slight external differences. Van Oordt, however, discovered a typical difference in their brooding instinct: the former begins to sit directly after laying her first egg, while the latter does not do so before the whole clutch is complete. This has the result that the young chicken of the latter species are all of the same size, while in the former there are differences in size. It was only at the beginning of this century that De Winton's yellow-necked mouse (Apodemus flavicollis Wintoni) was distinguished from the common field mouse (Apodemus sylvaticus sylvaticus) as a separate variety. As Frances Pitt remarks, a clear difference between the two, more marked than the morphological ones, is found in the fact that the latter never, or hardly ever, invades dwellings while the former is very fond of doing so. Thus many examples might be quoted in which instincts yield us a better criterion of a species than morphological characteristics. More important, however, for an understanding of instinct is the general fact that instincts are characteristic of the species, not of the individual.

This resemblance between the morphological or physiological structure and the instinctive outfit of an animal, the fact that both are specific and not individual in character, brings us to the question *whether there is a mutual connection between this morphological structure and these instincts*, and if so, which of them then is primary and which is dependent upon the other. That in many cases such a connection exists, nobody will deny. Without spinnerets no spider would be able to spin a web and without well-developed wings no bird could migrate to the South. The influence of hormones, especially of the sex hormones, on the instinctive behaviour of adult animals is beyond all doubt. But does this mean that instincts are the outcome of the animal's morphological structure or physiological functions, as has been asserted in times when psychical phenomena were not held in high esteem ? Is it true, as has been asserted by Müller-Erlangen, that an instinct is nothing more than the need to use an organ that the animal possesses ? Already the philosopher von Hartmann has combatted this view. All spiders possess the same spinning-glands ; yet some of them make a regular orb-web and others an irregular web, while yet others live in holes they only line with their spinnings. Further, this admission at best would explain why an animal uses an organ, but not the way in which it uses it ; that for instance the spider empties her spinning-glands, not that she weaves a web with their secretion. As Morgan remarked, nobody from the bodily structure of the eel would deduce the remarkable migration of these animals, nor from the anatomy of the ant-lion conclude that it makes a pit and there lies in wait for ants to fall down. On the other hand, similar instincts are shown by animals with quite a different bodily structure. Ants and termites, it is known, although belonging to quite different orders of insects, show a remarkable correspondence in their social instincts. Yet more striking perhaps is the resemblance, to which Wheeler has drawn our attention, between the instincts of the ant-lion and the worm-lion. The latter, the larva of the Dipteron Vermileo, is an animal which, with an entirely different bodily structure from that of the ant-lion, also makes a pit in the sand by throwing the sand up, lies there in wait for small insects which it pulls under the sand if they fall down into the pit, and also throws sand up if the prey tries to escape.

That there exists a connection between instinct and bodily structure nobody will deny ; that on the other hand the instincts are determined by the bodily structure cannot be maintained. We must consider them both as two different aspects of one phenomenon that lies at the background of both, and is realized in the structure as well as in the instinct. This basic phenomenon is empirically unknowable to us. Speculations as to its nature would lead us into the realm of metaphysics and cannot therefore find a place here.

Another characteristic of instinct and instinctive actions is the fact that they are *innate* and the actions *not acquired during lifetime*, be it by imitation or trial or by instruction from older members of the species. It has often been proved that animals reared in isolation from their congeners showed normal instincts and normal instinctive activity when the time for these had arrived. Young birds of prey, reared in isolation and always fed by hand, showed on the first occasion the same way of attacking and killing a prey as their congeners grown up in normal circumstances. Birds, bred in nests of other species, built a nest typical of their own species, so showing that they were not influenced by any remembrance of the nest in which they had spent the first days of their life. A young moorhen, reared in isolation by Morgan, was swimming in a pool when it was frightened by a young yelping dog. It then at once dived, and swam away under water as if it had learnt this way of flight from older moorhens. Typical instinctive actions, further, do not change in principle with repetition : the first web of the young spider is built after the same pattern as that of the old one, although of smaller dimensions. And all those instinctive actions of insects and other animals often so complicated and performed but once in their life, such as those connected with the propagation of the species, are carried out in their characteristic way by all members of the species without any tuition from their parents, which, as a rule, are already dead when the young ones arrive at the age to perform these acts.

Characteristic of the instincts is therefore that they are innate and not acquired. This, however, does not mean that all instincts are manifested directly after the birth of the animal. This will at once be clear of instincts that require a certain bodily development of the animal before coming into action. Birds that are not yet able to fly cannot fly away if danger is menacing, but will press themselves down and keep as motionless as possible, while their mother flies away. Instinctive actions connected with the propagation of the species will not show themselves before the animal has reached sexual maturity. Instinctive actions of animals that have to pass through a metamorphosis cannot be performed by the larva. All such instincts that show themselves only after a certain development of the animal were called by Morgan "deferred instincts."

The most interesting cases of these deferred instincts are those in which the delay of execution is not caused by a bodily development but by psychical maturation. A good example of this is provided by the division of labour in the bee-hive.

It was formerly believed that the different activities of the bees in the hive, such as the care for the brood, the building of the comb, the collecting of food and so on, were carried out by different groups of bees, so that the whole population was composed of different castes, each with its own task. Careful observations of Roesch, however, have shown that this is not the case, but that, on the contrary, every bee in the hive has during its lifetime to pass through all the different jobs. First, in the first ten days of their life, the young bees have the task to attend to the brood, to clean the cells in which the queen will deposit her eggs, to warm the developing brood by sitting on it, to feed the older larvæ with honey and pollen from the store-cells, and, when eventually their own food-glands have developed, to feed the young larvæ with the secretion of those glands. Then, in the second period, running from their tenth to twentieth day, they have other occupations, such as to take the food from the returning bees and bring it to the store-cells, to clean the hive and, further, to build the comb when their wax-glands have fully developed, which happens between the tenth and the seventeenth day. Finally, in the third period, which runs from the twentieth day up to their death, which in summer occurs between the thirtieth and thirty-fifth day, the bee works as a field-bee, collecting food and bringing it to the hive.

It is clear that we have here a number of examples of deferred instincts : although they are all innate, many of the instinctive actions of the bee are executed only at a certain age. It is also clear that in some of these cases there is a clear connection between the execution of the instinctive actions and bodily development. The feeding of the young larvæ with the bee's own feeding-juice has to wait for the full functioning of the feeding-glands ; the building of the comb for that of the wax-glands. Yet it would be wrong to believe that the appearance of all these instincts is determined by bodily development alone.

This was shown in a very interesting experiment by Roesch, in which he succeeded in dividing a population of bees into two groups of different ages : one younger and one older than eighteen days old. The result of this division was that in the younger population the menace of famine arose, as the foraging bees were wanting. Then, after some days, young bees of 7—15 days old flew out in search of food. At first they were still in possession of food-glands, and so flew out "physiologically precociously." In adaptation to the abnormal circumstances the population was thus split up into two groups of the same age with different occupations. On the other hand, in the group of older bees there arose a menace to the care of the brood, till some older bees took this task upon themselves. Also bees older than the normal builders began to build on the comb, and to that end even developed new wax-glands. Here, therefore, we have a case where the instinctive activity is certainly not dependent upon bodily development, but, on the contrary, bodily development is adapted to the psychological wants of the individual. Roesch further made the important observation that bees which had been isolated during the first ten days of their life, when brought back to the hive first went through the activities they had missed during their absence and so had to work off the arrears. This again shows that the instincts are relatively independent of bodily development and that the influence of mental maturity is an overriding one.

Now it is a curious fact that instincts which for their full realization require a special kind of bodily or psychical development, may, before this maturity has been reached, sometimes show themselves in a more or less schematic form and towards an object other than the adequate one. Young animals of prey, still nourished by their mother, practise their hunting instinct on a living or lifeless prey; young animals not yet sexually mature treat their brothers and sisters in a schematical way as sex partners. Herring-gulls sometimes show a sham nest-building, which precedes the real building of the nest ; the birds then pick up all sorts of material for nest-building in their beak, only to lay it down at another place without further attention to it. Howard observed with the whitethroat that the female one day takes some blades of grass in her beak but directly lets them fall again. The next day she carries the blades somewhat longer with her ; the following day she deposits a number of them in the fork of a branch ; some days later again she builds the beginning of a nest, till, finally, after having built such unfinished nests at different places, the final nest is built. Here we see before our eyes the maturation of an instinct and its development from a first tentative utterance up to its full expression. Much of what has been described as play in animals finds its explanation as a premature execution of instinctive activity. Groos, in his classic book on animal play, has stressed the value of such premature instinctive activities as a practice for later serious occupations. It is by no means certain, however, that the animal really requires such practice ; certainly the normal maturation of its instincts is by itself sufficient to enable the animal to execute the movements concerned with the necessary skill. Anyhow, these premature instinctive activities again show the relative independence of the instincts from bodily development.

We have already seen that Romanes in his definition of instinct pointed to two characteristics of instinctive actions to wit, that they are adaptive in character, i.e. generally purposeful, and are executed without the animal knowing the relation between the means employed and the end attained ; in other words that they are executed under the urge of a blind drive. This purposiveness presupposes a definite end towards which instinctive actions are directed. This, now, is an *essential characteristic* of instincts ; *their activity is all directed towards one special vitally important end,* be it the propagation of the species or the preservation of life, or something else. By this characteristic instinctive activity is distinguished from other forms of activity that, although innate, are not directed towards such an end. Activities like swimming, flying, creeping, diving, burrowing, and the like, are innate and in the special way in which they are performed often typical of the species of larger groups of animals. Yet as such, they are not directed to one special end. A water-bird may dive in order to escape or to seek for food ; a bird may fly for migrating, or in search of material to build its nest. On the other hand the escape of a water-bird may take place with the help of flying, of swimming or of diving. For this reason it would be erroneous to regard these general motor mechanisms as instinctive actions, as is sometimes done, only because they are innate and typical of the species. They are the means with which instincts are executed, not instinctive actions themselves. The directiveness of an instinct to one special end is an important feature of it.

This fact, namely, that instincts are all directed to a special end, puts the means into our hands to build up a *system of instincts.* It has sometimes been asked how many instincts some animal, or group of animals, possesses. This question cannot be answered so long as it has not been determined what is to be regarded as a unit of instinct. May we speak of one brood-caring instinct of the fossorial wasp, or must we distinguish in this animal a digging-instinct, a hunting-instinct, a paralyzing-instinct, a burying instinct, or perhaps even more subordinate instincts, which together form the care of the brood in the wasp ? According to Weyrauch no less than 57 different instincts are involved in the construction of the envelope of the nest in social wasps, every not farther analysable connection between a perception and a reaction being regarded as an independent instinct. In this way the animal instincts run into thousands ! It will be clear that instead of trying to enumerate in such a way the instincts of animals, it is much more convenient to construct a system of them, consisting of larger groups embracing smaller ones. By so doing the survey of animal instincts is facilitated.

If, therefore, in order to construct such a system, we ask what is the end towards which instincts are directed, we may say that in general they are all directed towards *the one great end of self-maintenance*, be it that of *individual self-maintenance*, the maintenance of the individual life, or that of *maintenance of the species*, the maintenance of the life of the species. This brings us to a first classification of instincts into two principal groups. Both of them in their turn may be divided into three sub-groups. The instincts of personal self-maintenance may be divided into those in service of bodily development, of self-sustenance and self-defence. The first sub-group embraces all instincts that lead the larvæ to activities necessary for their metamorphosis, such as the seeking for a proper place for pupation, the weaving of a cocoon, the digging into the soil by larvæ of Poly-chaetæ ; further, the opening of the egg-shell by the young bird at the moment of hatching, etc. The second sub-group comprises a great number of instincts that are all related to the satisfying of bodily wants, such as the seeking for water and hunting for food, the attacking of the prey and the killing of it, the seeking for a place for sleep, etc. Even so simple an action as the pecking up of a grain by a bird must be regarded as an instinctive activity belonging to this class. Many, more complicated, actions of other animals too belong to this sub-group : the construction of the pit by the ant-lion, and of the web by the spider as means to catch a prey. To the third group, that directed to the defence of life, belong all instincts of self-defence against an enemy, of flight in danger, the so-called instinct of "death-feigning," the instincts of migration or of hiding when the bad season approaches, the making of holes, or shelters, for protection, and several more. To this sub-group must also be reckoned the instinct of care for the body that many higher animals show, the aim of which is to keep the body in a good state of health (the so-called "comforting instinct"), like the cleaning of the body, the scratching induced by itching, etc., and further, the instinct of curiosity, an instinct that drives many animals (monkeys, rats, but also many birds) to examine new surroundings or an unknown object in them, the biological significance of which is to give the animal timely warning in case of eventual danger.

The second group, that of maintenance of the species, may also be divided into three sub-groups. These are that of propagation of the species, that of attending to the progeny and that of associating with congeners. To the first sub-group belong all instincts directed towards the winning of a sexual partner, as, for instance, the seeking and following of such a partner, the courtship, and so on, and further, all that belongs to the mating itself. The second sub-group comprises a great number of instinctive activities : that of making preparations for the laying of eggs or the delivery of their young, the building of nests and holes for the protection of the young ones, the breeding and defending of the eggs, the nourishing, caring and defending of the young, and so on. Finally, to the third sub-group belong all instinctive actions that are sometimes taken together under the head of one "social instinct." These are the instincts of keeping together with other animals of the same species, of communal attacking, hunting or defending, and so on, in short, all instincts that make social life in animals, be it in a herd of deer or a breeding colony of birds or a nest of ants or termites, possible and advantageous for the partners of such a union.

In this way we arrive, not at an infinite catalogue of instincts, but at a system, that is practically useful for the ordering of instincts, and at the same time giving us a survey on the manifold instinctive activities of animals. It is of course possible, and perhaps even necessary, to sub-divide again the instincts of the last sub-groups into smaller and more restricted sub-instincts and these again into groups that embrace yet simpler activities. We have not done this here because it would only be detrimental to the general surveyability. For the rest it will be clear that we shall not find all instincts, or even instincts of all these six classes, in every group of animals. It will, on the contrary, be the task of the student of animal behaviour to state what instincts each species of animal shows during the different phases of its life.

The characteristic of instincts, however, which has always struck most strongly the imagination of all observers, is not the fact that instincts are innate, or that they are typical for the species, but the fact that *instinctive activity in its whole complexity generally takes place so purposefully, although the animal executing these acts does not know, and often cannot even know, the end towards which its own actions are directed.* The latter is certainly the case with many of the instinctive activities that are related to the well-being of a progeny the animal will never see, and of the future existence of which it even has no idea. Let us imagine what passes in the feeble mind of a fossorial wasp, say a Sphex or an Ammophila, when setting out to procure provision for her future offspring. The only feeling she experiences at that moment is one of something in her body she will have to get rid of. That this something is an egg, i.e. a tiny little product of her genital glands, that will grow and develop into a living being, wanting for this development food and shelter, is of course something she does not know even on a second or third occasion, since she scarcely ever sees this egg and even then does not understand anything about the future history of such an object. Yet she flies out and behaves as if by careful study she had learnt that the egg would develop into a larva, and that this wanted food in the form of a paralysed grasshopper or caterpillar, and would now do her best to satisfy this want. The same holds true for simpler instinctive activities as well: the sitting of a bird on her eggs and even the sucking of the hungry newly-born mammal, that sucks at the breast of its mother, without possessing any knowledge of the function of lacteal glands and the physiology of nutrition.

This fact has led some philosophers to admit that instinct might include some, if not reflective then intuitive, knowledge of the world, and by this knowledge guide the animal to its goal. This view, however, is certainly untenable, if by intuitive knowledge we understand a real and explicit knowledge of things, not metaphysical wisdom. First of all, from a standpoint of science it is unthinkable how such an explicit intuitive knowledge could have been acquired by the animal in the course of evolution. But, above all, the animal often makes too many errors in executing instinctive actions to allow us to believe that it really possesses some knowledge of the end it is unconsciously pursuing. Spaier indeed admits that the instinct is not a knowledge but an innate knowing-how-to-act in a restricted number of cases, beyond which it may be stupid and awkward. Even this, however, if taken in the direct sense of the words, must either be rejected for the same reason we rejected the idea of intuition, or does not mean anything more than the acknowledgment that instinctive actions are purposeful to the end to which they are directed, and does not help us any farther.

Instincts, anyhow, may be said to compel animals to perform actions that are purposeful to the end towards which they are directed. This thesis scarcely needs any evidence. That the sucking of the young mammal is purposeful to the appeasing of its hunger, that the migration of the bird is purposeful to the preservation of its life during the bad season, that the weaving of the web by the spider is purposeful to the catching of insects, and the collecting and storing of caterpillars by the wasp purposeful to the nourishing of its future larva are facts that are so self-evident that it is not necessary further to elucidate them. More interesting and puzzling are the cases in which *instinctive actions lose their normal purposiveness and become futile, or even harmful to the animal.*

What may be the reason that in some circumstances instinctive actions lose their purposefulness ? The most fundamental cause again is the fact that instinctive actions are performed by the animal without knowledge of the end towards which they are directed. If the animal does not know to what end it performs actions, how can it leave off doing so in a case where they become inappropriate ? A striking example is reported by Hingston. Messor barbarus is an ant which collects seeds of grasses and carries them into the nest, where they are peeled and stored, after which the husks are carried out of the nest to a special refuse heap, about eight inches away from the nest. Hingston once found a nest that by way of exception was built in a vertical wall. Now the ants did not take advantage of the convenient position of the nest opening to throw the husks out, but continued carrying them eight inches away and laying them carefully against the wall, as if to make a heap there. Naturally the husks always fell down directly ; yet for months the ants continued doing this useless work. The deposition of the husks at a distance from the nest had become a no longer understood rite.

Hereby comes the fact that instinctive actions, if repeated for some time, show a tendency to rigidity, to become routine work ; the action then is executed without any discrimination of changes in the outer conditions. It is a well-known fact that if in the absence of the bees the hive be displaced a few metres, the old bees on their return assemble at the place where, before they left, the entrance of the hive had been, and only gradually find the new place of entrance. Their return to the hive then is controlled not by perception of its place, but by a routine act that now fails them. The most important reason, however, of such unpurposefulness of instinctive action lies in the fact that the *perception* that incites the instinctive action in many cases is *too indefinite* to give to the animal a discrimination between appropriate and inappropriate execution of this action.

Instincts, it must be remembered, do not unexpectedly and without any inducement come into full action, as Athena suddenly appeared in full armour from the head of Zeus. An instinct, as we shall have to illustrate presently, is evoked by a cognition, be it a simple sensation or a more complex perception. And it is in this initiating perception that the cause of an inappropriate functioning of an instinct is often to be found.

Observations and experiments in recent years have shown that in many cases the initiating perception is much simpler and much poorer in content, than one would suppose, and that for this reason it becomes a key that may open the door to a wrong road. Young chickens, for instance, as we know from Morgan's classic observations, in the first hours of their life do not pick only at grains of corn and other edible objects, but at any small object within their reach, so that they also pick at little pebbles, pieces of paper, the toes of their brothers, little spots of light on the ground and other not edible things. That experience of the good and bad effects of their picking speedily intervenes and leads the chicken to pick at edible objects is a question that does not concern us here. In this case the picking instinct, therefore, is released, not by the perception of small pieces of food, but by the much less definite, and much simpler perception of "a small object." New-born mammals do not only suck the teats of their mother, but anything warm and soft, so that young dogs may be observed sucking the tail or the ears of their mother, or the snout of one of their brothers. Hungry larvæ of dragonflies not only throw out their "mask" (their prehensile organ) towards moving insects, but to any not too large object moving in their neighbourhood, such as pieces of paper or even moving spots of light. The cause of all these errors lies in the imperfection of the releasing perception.

Other instincts than the feeding instinct are also sometimes misled by the too simple character of the releasing perception. The black-headed gull, according to Kirkman, sits not only on its own eggs and on those of ducks, but also on wooden eggs and little tins and balls, and even on pieces of coal—apparently on any object of small size. For the laying of their eggs insects are attracted by the smell of appropriate food for the larvæ. But often they are misled by similar odours given forth by wrong objects. Insects, for instance, that lay their eggs in putrefying flesh may also lay them in flowers with a similar scent, and the butterfly Papilio demolus that lays its eggs on orange trees does this, according to Vosseler, also on stones to the leeward of those trees that are impregnated by their odour. Lissmann observed that the first phase of the battle of the fighting fish Betta splendens can be released by the simple perception of a moving object of its own size, even by that of a cross with arms of 1 cm. large and 4-5 cm. long. Of a couple of partridges reared from the eggs by Heinroth, the female, when arrived at sexual maturity, treated her nurse as a sexual partner, while the cock showed a hostile disposition towards her, only because she wore a brown apron of the same colour as the breast fleck of the cock. Apparently the brown patch on his breast, not the cock as such, stirred the sexual instincts of both animals.

It would not be difficult to quote many more cases in which the all-too-simple character of the releasing perception, of the "releaser," as it is often called, is the cause of instincts working in an unpurposeful, or even detrimental way. It must be acknowledged, however, that in most of these cases this unpurposiveness is the fault of man, that great disturber of the harmony of nature, be it that by interfering with nature he creates conditions in which an instinct is apt to function in an inappropriate way, be it that he confuses the animal by teasing it with what he himself calls his "experiments." Hingston records that the Indian ant Camponotus compressus builds her nest at the foot of high trees. This is a suitable place for it, as the ant feeds herself on the juices of insects that live on the leaves of trees, so that she merely has to climb the trunk to arrive at the food. Since, however, man builds walls, nests also are found at the bottom of such walls, along which the ants go out in vain for food. The instinct to build a nest at the foot of a high object was purposeful only as long as such objects were trees. The new-born lamb of the sheep of the Pampas, according to Hudson, has the instinct to run away from every approaching object, and to follow every object that retreats. In the natural life of the herd this has the result that the young animal stays with the mother and so keeps in contact with the herd. In herds that are looked after by man, on the contrary, this has often the effect that the animal joins a departing shepherd, or horse, and so gets lost from the herd.

But it is especially by human experiments that animal instincts are often turned into caricatures. The caterpillars of the processionary moth Cnethocampa processionea owe their name to the fact that in the evening they leave the common nest in great numbers in search of food. Then they march in single file one after another, the head of each animal touching the back-end of the animal before, at the same time spinning a thread which, united to those of the others, forms a silken band. This band keeps the animals together and facilitates the way back to the nest. In this procession there is no special leader : any one that accidentally proceeds at the head of the column is slavishly followed by the others. Fabre now succeeded in letting the one in front fall in behind the one in the rear, whereupon it at once gave up its leading function and followed the animal before it. The result of this was that a ring was formed in which the animals kept marching on round and round for more than seven days. It was only on the eighth day that finally the ring was broken by some smaller groups. Fabre computed that they were in motion for at least 84 hours, and covered the circle about 355 times. A similar result was later obtained by Wheeler with the wandering ant Eciton schmitti.

It is therefore clear that for the efficient working of instinct it is necessary for the releasing perception to be so unequivocally determined that any erroneous reaction towards an inadequate stimulus is precluded. The examples just quoted show that this is not always the case. The indefiniteness of the perception, then, is the cause of the errors that so mar instincts. But it is better in such a case not to speak of errors ; as Russell rightly remarked, the animal does not make errors, but is misled.

One striking case in which in nature a beautiful and complicated instinct is led astray by the all-too-simple character of the releasing perception may be quoted from Fabre. The larvæ of the beetle Sitaris pass their development in the cells of the solitary bee Anthophora. To this end the Sitaris mother lays her eggs at the entrance of the nest of this bee. The young larvæ hibernate in these galleries, till in spring, when the larvæ are already seven months old, the young bees leave their nest. At that moment the Sitaris-larvæ attach themselves to the hairy bodies of the bees. Now these young bees are mostly males, as the males come out earlier than the females, and it therefore is necessary for the larvæ to go over on to the females, which can only take place at the moment of copulation. If this succeeds the larvæ attach themselves to the thorax of the female bee and try to pass over to an egg of Anthophora at the moment this is laid. If this also succeeds the larva can feed herself first on the egg and then on the contents of the cell of the Anthophora.

Now the value of this interesting instinct of the Sitaris-larva is, however, diminished by the fact that the perception which has to release the transition to the female Anthophora is too indefinite. Not only do the larvæ fail to distinguish sufficiently between a male and a female Anthophora, whereby many of them remain attached to bees of the wrong sex, but they even do not distinguish between an Anthophora and other insects, and attach themselves to wrong species, like flies or honey-bees. Fabre even observed that they may cling to inanimate hairy objects. In such cases they naturally perish, as for their further development they are strictly adapted to the life of Anthophora. Here again the releasing perception is not differentiated enough : it is not the perception of a female Anthophora, but of any hairy object moving along, which releases the act of attaching. That the number of eggs laid by the beetle is so great that it compensates this imperfection of the instinct, does not alter the fact that by this too-schematic character of the releasing perception the purposeful working of the instinct is often disturbed.

These cases, now, bring us to another point of importance. Is the animal, when performing an instinctive action, so strictly bound, so little capable of adaptive changes of its action, that it cannot by any means leave the road prescribed by its instincts so as to make its behaviour more appropriate to circumstances differing slightly from the normal ones ?

This question brings us to the much-discussed point of *the rigidity or suppleness of the instincts.*

Are instincts so rigid as not to allow any freedom of action to the animal if altered circumstances need some change in the normal instinctive behaviour ? Fabre indeed maintained this, not only for theoretical reasons, but also from the result of his experiments. Let us, therefore, describe some of these experiments and their results.

One experiment, often quoted, was the following. The fossorial wasp Sphex catches and paralyses grasshoppers, drags them to her nest and there buries them after having laid an egg on them. Before drawing the grasshopper into the nest she first lays it down at the edge of the nest and enters without it for a last inspection. If the nest is found to be in a good state, not occupied by another wasp or damaged in any way, she seizes her prey and draws it in. Fabre now, during such an inspection, removed the grasshopper some inches away from the nest. When the wasp after finishing her inspection came out and discovered the grasshopper at some distance from the nest, she drew it back to the edge of the nest again, but did not pull it in, and anew entered her nest for an inspection. Fabre took this opportunity to remove the grasshopper once more to some distance ; the wasp on coming out of the nest once more drew it to the edge of the nest and then again entered for an inspection. As Fabre then again laid the grasshopper aside, the wasp acted again as before. This little comedy was repeated some forty times ; then Fabre abandoned his experiment. The wasp, therefore, proved to be unable to bring a grasshopper directly into her nest if it lay at some distance from it, but had first to inspect the nest. In other words : the perception of a grasshopper lying at some distance from the nest impelled the wasp first to draw it to the edge of it, then to inspect the nest and only then to pull it in, even if she had inspected the nest just before. Or more generally : a special perception always released a special action, even if this action had become unnecessary and senseless.

In some other cases, too, in which, as often happens in complex instinctive activity, one part of the complex is executed only after a preceding part of it has been finished, it appeared that the connection between the two parts was so firm that the second part could only be performed in direct connection with the first. The mason-bee Chalicodoma muraria builds a cell from a mixture of earth and the secretion of her own salivary glands ; this cell is then filled with honey and pollen on which she lays her egg. When provisioning the cell the bee first goes forward into the cell to empty her crop filled with honey ; then she goes backward into it to wipe the pollen from her abdomen. Fabre now prevented a Chalicodoma from executing this second act by pushing her away with a straw at the moment she tried to enter the cell backwards. Then the bee again started to enter the cell in a forward direction, although her crop was now empty, and only after this tried to enter it backwards to get rid of the pollen. As this once more was prevented by Fabre, she again went head first into the cell, and so on. Ultimately the bee only partially entered the cell or merely put her head into it ; yet she was not able wholly to omit the first action before performing the second one. In this case the link between the two parts of an instinct-complex proved to be very rigid.

In many cases it was shown that if animals are performing one part of such an instinct-complex, they are not able to return to an earlier part of it. When a Chalicodoma was building her cell, Fabre made a hole in the bottom of it. The bee discovered and repaired the damage. When, however, the hole was made when the bee was collecting provision for the cell, she did not repair it, although she discovered the damage and touched the edges of the hole, but went on provisioning the damaged cell with honey and pollen, which were immediately lost through the hole. Finally she laid her egg in the empty cell. During and after the provisioning the bee, therefore, was not able to return to an earlier part of the instinctive complex, namely, building the cell.

It has not been Fabre only who observed such cases of rigidity of instincts. In a species of the wasp Ammophila, that brings more than one caterpillar in her nest, Ferton met one specimen that was just closing her nest after having brought in two caterpillars and having laid an egg on them. He then laid a caterpillar, paralysed by another wasp, close to the nest. When the wasp found this caterpillar she inspected it, laid it down at the edge of her nest and re-opened it. When she then found the nest already filled she closed it again, but then she found the caterpillar again, which induced her to open the nest anew. When for the second time she found the nest already filled she closed it definitely and flew away, anxiously avoiding the place where the paralysed caterpillar was lying. Although the rigidity of the instinct in this case was not so absolute as in the former cases, yet the perception of the paralysed caterpillar twice forced her again to open the nest she had herself just filled and closed.

An interesting case has been reported by Hingston. The solitary wasp, Eumenes conica, builds a dome-shaped cell and after finishing it fixes an egg in the top of the dome and provisions the cell with a number of small caterpillars. Hingston now cut away the top of the cell before an Eumenes had laid her egg in it. The wasp at once noticed the lack of the normal place for the egg and, although within the dome there was plenty of room to fix her egg, she could not bring herself to lay the egg on any other than the usual place, so that after some vain efforts she laid it there, where the top of the cell should be, with the result that the egg was shot into the air and lost.

Most descriptions of such a rigidity of instinct are concerned with insects. But higher animals may also sometimes provide examples of such an incapacity for changing innate behaviour in cases that deviate but slightly from the normal. When the viper Vipera aspis finds a mouse, she bites her, lets her go and after some time follows her trail till she finds the dead mouse and swallows her. Baumann in an experiment changed the bitten mouse for a fresh one. When the viper found her, the fresh mouse was not bitten but treated as if this had happened already. The mouse then defended herself against the viper and in many cases succeeded in escaping. Only if the mouse in defending herself jumped on the viper was she bitten. There was nothing to prevent the viper from biting again, but the rigidity of its hunting instinct was such that it prevented it biting a mouse more than once, even if this was necessary.

Even birds sometimes give proof of an amazing rigidity in their instincts. With breeding pigeons the parent birds relieve each other at a fixed hour of the day : the female sits from the later afternoon till the next morning ; the male from the morning till the afternoon. Lorenz, now, once watched a pair of pigeons of which the female was killed by a cat. The male then did not brood longer than normally, went out for food at the time the female had to relieve him and did not sit on the nest the night, but beside it. As the night was cold the young died. Nevertheless, next morning the male sat on the dead bodies of the young ones till the afternoon. For two days this senseless behaviour continued. Here, again, the animal showed an incapacity to adapt its behaviour to changed conditions and was not able to desist in an action that had lost its purpose.

It would be wrong, however, to believe that with these examples of rigidity of an instinct the last word on this question has been said. On the contrary, as many examples of the opposite kind might be quoted.

First of all, other observers, when repeating Fabre's experiments, did not always find the same proofs of a rigidity of instinct as Fabre had found. When the Peckhams, with another Sphex, repeated Fabre's experiment of removing the grasshopper, the wasp after four times dragging the grasshopper to the edge of the nest, the fifth time drew it straight into the nest. To tell the truth, even Fabre, when repeating his own experiment another year with another Sphex, found that after some two or three times this wasp also drew the grasshopper straight into the nest. The same was the case with a Pompilus, with whom Ferton tried Fabre's experiment. And when Ferton repeated the experiment he had before done with Ammophila, and laid a paralysed spider beside the closed nest of a Pompilus, a species of fossorial wasp that collects spiders in her nest, the wasp, after finding the new spider, did not open her nest again, but dug a new hole and buried the spider in it, after having laid its egg on it.

Also Hingston, who reports so many instances of rigidity

of instincts, found cases of suppleness in the working of instincts where Fabre had found none. We have already mentioned that Fabre's Chalicodoma did not repair a hole made in her cell while she was filling it with honey, but went on filling it as if nothing had happened. When Hingston did the same with an Eumenes that had flown out in search of caterpillars, the first caterpillar brought back by the wasp fell down through the hole. A second one was caught just hanging partly in and partly outside of the cell. At first the wasp did not pay attention to the damage, but when she had brought in enough caterpillars she inspected the hole, pushed the hanging caterpillar with great trouble into the cell and flew away to fetch sand to close the hole.

A rigidity as asserted by Fabre, therefore, is certainly not the rule in instinctive behaviour. On the contrary, a closer examination of the instinctive behaviour of insects, spiders and other animals has shown that there are three groups of facts that stand out in contrast to this idea of their absolute rigidity. First, there is the great *variability* in instincts and instinctive actions. Then, instincts in many cases show *adaptation* to small changes in the external conditions. And, finally, they often show a *regulation* of behaviour that goes farther than simple adaptation. Let us now consider some instances of these three aspects of instinctive life.

First a few words concerning this *variability of instincts*. Nearly all investigators who after Fabre studied the instinctive life of animals, have emphasized the fact that although instincts in general follow a fixed schema, yet in details instinctive actions show a variability that is incompatible with the idea of their absolute fixedness. Especially the Peckhams, in contrast to Fabre, have always laid stress on this variability even in the behaviour of fossorial wasps, of which Fabre quoted so many instances of rigid behaviour. Never, according to them, are two nests of Ammophila entirely similar ; never do we observe in them exactly the same way of digging a hole, of paralysing a caterpillar, of dragging the prey to the nest. One time the caterpillars in the nest will be dead, another time they are alive and well or only slightly paralysed. According to Hingston, Sphex lobatus on one occasion stings her prey only once, on another two to five times. With Eumenes we shall sometimes find four paralysed caterpillars in the nest ; at others eight to ten. As a rule the wasp lays one egg in each cell ; sometimes, however, we find nests without any egg or with three. And when we come to the instinctive behaviour of higher animals, like birds and mammals, the variability is so great that if often seems as if their actions are not ruled by any leading instinct at all. It will be clear that, although all such variations themselves are of minor importance and follow the general rule of variability of all vital phenomena, yet they are contrary to the idea of an absolute rigidity of innate instincts.

More important as an evidence against their absolute rigidity are the *adaptations* instincts often show if required by special circumstances. If the normal material for a nest, or the normal prey, is not available, the animal often knows how to manage with other objects. The fossorial wasp Pelopaeus hunts spiders of the genus Epeira, but if these are not to be found she may catch other ones. The parasitic bee Osmia lines her cell with the petals of flowers ; Osmia papaveris does this with the red petals of the poppy. Ferton now found that in Corsica, where this flower is lacking, the wasp uses the yellow petals of Glaucium luteum, and in the Pyrenees the blue petals of Malva. The same Osmia builds her nest in holes in wood or in the spaces between stones, by preference, however, in the empty shells of snails. Then the form of the nest is adapted to the available space : in long stalks the cells are placed in one long row, in openings between stones in an irregular heap, in snail-shells cells are built in a simpler row in the narrower convolutions of the shell, while nearer to the opening of the shell the cells are laid side by side. Even the very stereotyped form of the web of the spider may be more or less modified if the available space requires an adaptation of it.

Now even these adaptations are mostly not very radical deviations from the normal instinctive course, although it would be difficult to reconcile them with the idea of strict rigidity. More decisive, therefore, are the cases in which animals, in executing instinctive actions, prove to be able to change their behaviour if important changes in the conditions demand this. The clearest instances of such *regulations* we find where an animal is under the necessity of *repairing damaged constructions*.

We have already mentioned two cases with contradictory results. Fabre's Chalicodoma did not repair its damaged cell while at work provisioning it ; Hingston's Eumenes did, after first proceeding with its provisioning. The former wasp, therefore, was not able to break off her normal behaviour and return to a preceding link in the chain of instinctive actions ; the latter showed a regulative change in it. With another Eumenes that already had filled her cells and had laid her eggs on the collected caterpillars, and that was now beginning to build a cover of mud around it, Hingston opened one cell and took the caterpillars away. At first the wasp went on working on the cover ; after a dozen journeys, however, she began to repair the damage. When this was done she came back with a caterpillar, started again with provisioning and finally finished her normal task.

More important and complete in this respect were the results Verlaine obtained with a Pelopæus, a fossorial wasp of the Congo. In imitation of Fabre, he partially destroyed the cells of these wasps at different stages, took the collected spiders away, and so forth, to see if the wasps would be able to repair the damage. It was only seldom that the wasps went on as if nothing had happened ; in 86 out of 91 cases they did mend the damage. A hole in the side of the cell was repaired when this had been made during the building of the cell, or when the cell was ready, or when the egg was laid, or even when the wasp discovered the damage when she was already working at the provisioning of a new cell. If Verlaine gave her a cell filled with spiders, the wasp at once commenced closing it. If her egg was taken away, the wasp laid a new one ; if the spider with the egg was removed, the wasp brought in a new spider and laid an egg on it. In all this behaviour the normal sequence of actions, namely, the building of the cell, the bringing in of a spider, the laying of an egg, the provisioning of the cell with more spiders and the final closing of the cell, was broken off by the wasp ;

she was able to return from a later to an earlier action and also to omit an action which was part of the regular sequence. Of a fixed rigidity of the instinctive behaviour here no trace could be observed.

A construction that often served as an object for experiments on the rigidity, or suppleness, of instinct is the web of the spider. Does the spider repair her web after damage, or not ?

To understand these experiments better we must first say a few words on the way a cobweb is constructed. In the common garden spider Epeira this in brief takes place in the following way. The spider begins by constructing a framework of threads, first of triangular form but afterwards made irregularly quadrilateral by spinning a horizontal thread within the triangle. From the centre of this framework she then spins a number of radii, or spokes, alternately on opposite sides of the centre, and making almost equal angles with each other. The number of these spokes varies with the species, each species of spider having its own fixed number. Then, in the centre, these radii are connected together by other threads, forming an irregular texture : the hub. When this is ready the spider constructs a provisional spiral of ordinary thread, spun from the hub outwards to the circumference and passing from one spoke to the next one. The function of this provisional spiral is to serve as a scaffolding for the spider when she makes her final, or viscid, spiral that serves to hold the insects that are unhappy enough to fly into the web ; this final spiral, in contrast to the provisional one, is spun from the periphery to the centre of the web. In spinning this final spiral the spider uses the provisional one to cross over from one radius to the next one. The viscid spiral differs from the provisional one by being provided with viscid globules by which the insects are held. When the viscid spiral is ready, the spider destroys the provisional one. Finally round the centre a notched zone is constructed in which she sits awaiting the prey that will fly into the web. In some species we find slight deviations from this general schema, which it is not necessary to enter into here.

Fabre cut the web of an Epeira into two. The spider,

when returning to her web, discovered the damage, since she no longer found support for her legs on one side. She then spun two threads from the hub to the other side of the breach, but did not repair the web and kept sitting on the remaining half. In another experiment he cut away the whole viscid spiral of a web. Then, too, the spider did no repairs, but kept sitting on a web consisting only of the remaining radii. Hingston came to similar results with the spider Araneus nauticus. When the spider was weaving her viscid spiral he, in one sector of the web, cut away one or two parts of the provisional spiral. Although the spider seemed to notice the absence of the threads she did not replace them, but went on to an inner winding of the spiral to pass from there to the next radius. When Hingston destroyed all the parts of the provisional spiral in one sector of the web, the spider did not lay new bridges between the radii, but every time she came to that sector she went to the hub to reach the next radius. And when he destroyed all connecting threads between the radii, the spider went every time from the periphery to the centre, and from there back to the periphery, rather than build a new provisional spiral. The result of this behaviour was an entirely irregular web with threads partly sticking together.

The conclusion to be drawn from these experiments would seem to be that the spider does not repair her web if it is damaged after being once finished, and even does not repair damage made while she is engaged in another part of her web-building activity.

Once again, however, other experiments had different results. In particular it appeared that the radii of the web are easily repaired, probably because the perception of the loss of the tension of the web induces the spider to rebuild them. Hingston found that if during the weaving of the web a new radius was removed, the spider replaced the removed radius by a new one as often as 25 times. Wiehle and Peters found also that, if during the weaving of the web the tension was much disturbed, for instance by cutting through the framework or taking away one of the spanning threads, the spider repaired the damage by making new threads. If a large part of the web was taken away, Peters observed that not only radii and threads of the framework, but even the viscid spiral might be repaired. Lesser damages of the web, according to Peters, are repaired if made by the spider herself, for example when she loosens the prey from the place where she has spun it in, in order to suck it out in the centre of the web.

The results Verlaine obtained with young spiders of the genus Epeira, only a few millimetres in length, go yet further. If in this case the provisional spiral was destroyed, this was wholly or partially repaired, even when the spider was already working at her viscid spiral. If in two sectors of the web all provisional threads were taken away, they were replaced by some irregular threads and then the viscid spiral completed. If the whole provisional spiral, and the first viscid thread, were removed, the spider built a new web on the old radii. If a great number of radii were removed, the spider went so far as to demolish the already completed part of the viscid spiral, the provisional spiral and sometimes even the remaining radii, to build a new web in the old framework. With such young spiders Verlaine therefore found a much greater power of regulation of the instinctive behaviour than had been found by other authors with older ones.

That instinct is not so rigid as has been supposed, has thus been made clear for the web-building of the spider. But now the question arises how it can be that different experimenters obtain such different and contradictory answers with regard to the question of the rigidity or suppleness of instinct, and that, e.g., Hingston might be quoted for, as well as against, both views. Of course it must be taken into account that they often worked with different species and not always under quite the same circumstances. But there must be yet another reason for their differing results. It seems probable that there are periods in animal life when the animal is more susceptible to outer impressions, and therefore more supple in its behaviour than during other periods. Especially the youth of an animal, or rather the period in which an instinctive action is performed for the first time or one of the first times, seems to be a period in which deviations from the innate succession of actions are easier than at a later time. It is significant in this respect that Verlaine, who obtained the strongest evidence for the suppleness of instinct, worked with quite young animals, while others, like Fabre, probably worked with older ones. In later life the activity has lost its youthfulness, has become more or less a routine-action, from which it is more difficult for the animal to deviate. But besides this, it is probable that during the unwinding of the chain of instinctive actions there are moments of greater and lesser suppleness and rigidity coinciding with fluctuations in the attention of the animal which is sometimes more intensely directed to the work it is executing (to the exclusion of what is happening around it) than at others. We have already seen that Hingston's Eumenes did not at first repair the damage done to its cell, but when she had finished with her provisioning she paid attention to it and began to close the hole ; in another experiment by the same author she first finished making the cover of her cells and then started anew to repair the damaged cell and fill it with caterpillars. It may be possible, therefore, that adaptations to changes in the situation are lacking, simply because these changes did not attract the animal's attention, were not observed by it.

An interesting case of this variation in the attention given to changes in the situation was reported by Baerends. He worked with Ammophila campestris, a species that differs from other Ammophila-species in that it makes two nests at the same time, and after having brought one caterpillar into each of them and having laid an egg on it, further provisions the nests according to needs. For this she opens her nest for an inspection, at first without bringing a caterpillar with her. If it then appears that the developing larva wants more food, she brings in more caterpillars.   Baerends now found that at this inspection the wasp takes notice of any striking changes in her nest and adaptively reacts to them. If, for instance, the larva has been taken out of the nest, or a living larva replaced by a dead one, or if the larva has been replaced by an undeveloped egg, the wasp stops further provisioning. If, on the other hand, the egg has been replaced by a larva, the wasp at once starts provisioning. If the experimenter augmented the number of caterpillars in the nest, the wasp herself brought in only a few ; if, instead of a growing larva a spinning larva or a cocoon was brought into the nest, the wasp closed it without provisioning it further. In all these cases the behaviour of the wasp showed adaptive regulation to the situation noted : the opening of a cell was not blindly followed by provisioning, whether necessary or not. Quite different, however, was the case when the wasp had already commenced upon the provisioning itself. If then the larva was taken out of the nest or replaced by an egg, the wasp continued bringing in new caterpillars ; if every time the new caterpillar was taken away, the number of caterpillars brought in was no larger than usual, and then the nest was closed. During this provisioning all regulation was absent, and the rigidity of the action once started stood out clearly.

But it is time now to come to a conclusion about the rigidity, or suppleness, of instinct. This conclusion must be that *this rigidity is certainly not so fundamental a character of instinctive behaviour as was formerly believed.* By nature an instinct is more or less supple, and it is only when an instinctive action has been repeated several times, that the original suppleness may give place to a greater or less rigidity. Rigidity, then, must be regarded as a sign that the instinct has aged, or as the result of flagging interest for, and attention to, changes in the environment. It goes without saying that this suppleness, on the other hand, must not be overrated : the instinctive behaviour follows the schema of the innate instinct, and we may as little expect an ant-lion to come out of its pit to chase insects as a tiger to get aversion to killing living animals, and be converted to the eating of fruits and grass.

One more question about this suppleness must, however, be answered. How must we understand these regulative adaptations of animals to changes in the situation ? Must we regard them as a proof of *intelligence* and ascribe them to an *intelligent insight* on the part of the animal ?

Some students of animal instinct have indeed done so.

This, however, cannot be right. First of all, as we will see in a later chapter, insight is a faculty of mind only to be found in higher animals, not with the animals in which we here found these examples of suppleness in instinct : the insects and spiders. Further, such an insight presupposes a conscious knowledge of the end to be attained and the means necessary to obtain it, and we saw that at the level of instinctive behaviour such a knowledge is and often must be wanting. If we admit insight in the case of adaptive regulation of behaviour, the errors of instinct in other similar cases remain inexplicable. If there is insight in instinct, this insight is of a supra-individual, not to say a metaphysical, nature. But we prefer to reserve the term insight to individual performances, and not to class all cases of teleological behaviour under the concept of insight. For the explanation of such regulative adaptations therefore we shall have to look *into the concept of instinct itself.*

In doing so, we shall have to admit that within the range of instinctive activity there are more possibilities than can be discovered by simple observation alone. The perception of the cell-in-the-making evokes in Eumenes the action of fetching sand and building further on it ; the perception of a hole in the finished cell evokes the action of fetching sand and repairing the hole. The perception of a nest wanting some caterpillars evokes in Ammophila campestris the action of hunting for caterpillars ; once her attention is focussed on the fact that there is not a larva but a cocoon in the nest, this perception induces her to close the nest, although otherwise she would have gone on provisioning it. And, likewise, once the attention of Verlaine's young spiders is drawn to the fact that the provisional spiral is missing, this discovery brings them to stop spinning the viscid spiral and to recommence building the provisional one. The laying of another egg if the first one has been taken away is induced in Pelopæus by the perception that the egg is missing on the spiders ; egg laying, therefore, is not only evoked by the perception that she has filled her cell with spiders. The same holds true for the little adaptations cited above : the adaptation of the form of the nest of Osmia to the room available, the accepting of an abnormal prey if the normal victim is wanting, and so forth.

On the other hand, just as different perceptions may give rise to similar actions, similar perceptions may evoke different actions. We have already spoken of the variability observed by several students in the instinctive activity of fossorial wasps. The perception of the cell to be filled sometimes evokes in Eumenes the collecting of four caterpillars, another time of eight or ten. The perception of the nest to be closed, according to the Peckhams, may once incite Ammophila to lay a clump of earth on it, another time to put a little stone into it and to fill it up with sand ; again another time to lay two clods of sand just in the opening and to cover them with smaller clods and sand.

It therefore becomes clear that at both ends of the instinctive chain, on the side of the perception as well as on the side of the action, there may be *some margin, some breadth*, that allows of variations in the normal course, adaptations to small changes in the surroundings, and a regulative change where the conditions require it. We have already pointed out, however, that one must not overestimate the possibilities of this instinct-breadth. We must also keep in mind that there are differences in this breadth of instinct, differences between the different instincts of one animal as well as differences in the same instinct of different animals. The herring-gull, which is omnivorous and feeds itself with nearly everything it finds on the beach, with the eggs and young of other birds, and the waste from the tables of man, has a much broader feeding instinct than the tern, which catches its food only by diving into the water. In song-birds the nest-building instinct shows greater breadth than the feeding-instinct : the individual nests of such birds, therefore, show greater difference than the food they eat. In general we may say that the higher the animal, the wider its instincts. So the instincts of birds and mammals generally are wider and less definite than those of insects and spiders. We may say that in insects the instincts determine not only the ends but also the means ; in the higher animals little more than the ends are determined. This is the reason why in higher animals instincts are more easily overlooked than in the lower ones, and their rôle in the behaviour of the higher animals is often underestimated. As we shall see in a later chapter, this breadth of instinct is of great importance in the acquisition of experience and the working of intelligence.

Before ending these general remarks on instincts and instinctive actions we must say a few words regarding a curious feature of this activity, recently discovered by Kortlandt and by Tinbergen. If, for some reason the normal issue of an instinctive activity is interrupted, the energy, set free by the drive, may "spark over" to another movement mechanism and so seemingly evoke another instinct, for which there is no motive at that moment. For instance : two male birds meet at the boundary of their breeding territory and there make threatening movements at each other as a preliminary to a fight ; yet they do not proceed to actual fighting, but begin to pick up food or nest-material, in which, however, in reality no food is swallowed and the bill of the bird often does not even reach the ground. The reason why the fighting instinct was suppressed is to be found in the antagonistic instinct of flight, released by the perception of the opponent on the boundary of his own territory and ready to defend it. Another reason of such a sparking over of energy may be found in the fact that the end of an instinctive action has been reached too soon, so that there remains a residue of unused psychical energy. This may happen if the opponent evades the fight by flight. Then the victor often pretends to pick up food, bathe, clean his feathers, and the like. Hitherto most of the examples of such "sparking-over movements," or "*displacement reactions*," as they are also called, are found in birds, but there are indications that they may also be found in higher animals, perhaps even in man. The origin of this sparking-over of energy, the function of which must be to provide a means of discharge for a not wholly realized drive, remains obscure.

In the foregoing pages we have described the general characteristics of instincts : their specificity, their innateness, their directiveness, their purposefulness. We further discussed their rigidity and suppleness. We will now endeavour shortly to pass in review the principal forms of instinct found in the animal world.

We have already pointed to the fact that an instinct does not come into action without some preceding cause, but is evoked by a *cognition* of some kind. What is the character of this cognition, and are there differences in the nature and degree of complexity of instinctive actions, correlated with the nature and complexity of their releasing cognition ?

Here we must first make a distinction between a *cognition of inner, and one of outer, origin*. Instinctive actions are sometimes evoked by inner cognitions, sometimes by outer ones, often by both. In these *inner cognitions* we may group all bodily sensations, like hunger, thirst, fatigue, sexual stimulation, etc., evoked by special changes in the body. Here we must sharply distinguish, however, between the initial sensation and the agreeable, or disagreeable, feeling that follows it : the sensation of an empty stomach or the sensation of weakness caused by the fact that no food has been eaten for some time, is quite different from the feeling of discomfort or pain that sooner or later follows this sensation. These inner sensations now evoke a striving, directed to the appeasement of these bodily wants. If this is achieved, if an object is perceived suited to satisfy the want, a second phase is initiated which for the moment does not interest us here. The actions evoked by this striving to appease bear the character of spatially undirected searching activities. The hungry animal, experiencing the bodily sensation of hunger and the feeling of discomfort caused by it, goes in search of food till an adequate object is found with which to satisfy its hunger. The same is the case with the animal which experiences thirst, or is sexually stimulated, and the same with the insect that feels in itself the urge to lay eggs (i.e., experiences the sensation of having eggs to get rid of), and again with the caterpillar that experiences the sensation of being ripe for pupation, and so on. Perhaps only the tired animal, experiencing the sensation of bodily exhaustion, is usually not obliged to seek for a suitable place to rest but can lie down where it is. Yet for their night-rest many animals have to seek for a suitable place.

It is not necessary to quote instances of such a seeking-behaviour, evoked by inner sensations, in the higher animals. As to the lower ones, we have already seen in the first chapter in this book that if Amoeba has been suspended in the water for some time without contact with a fixed object, it stretches out its pseudopodia to all sides in search for such an object to attach itself to. If this object is found, the second phase of the behaviour is initiated, and the animal goes over to it. It is probable the feeling of hunger that incites Hydra, after it has remained quietly in one place for a long time, to leave this and crawl round till it fixes itself at another place in the aquarium. And even in the case of the ant-lion, that, as we saw before, was regarded by Doflein solely as a reflex machine, Doflein could not help stating that when the animal has been waiting for some time in vain for a prey, it becomes restless and moves away till at another place it starts again to build a new pit. In the figures Doflein gives of the path described by the animals in these locomotor activities, in which circles and spirals are drawn by the animals, the lack of spatial directiveness of these seeking-movements is clearly expressed.

Now it is an interesting fact that, if such inner drives are very strong, if the animal is very hungry, or very strongly sexually stimulated, or very much driven by a need to breed, and the appropriate object to appease this drive is lacking, the perception which is able to release the second phase of the instinctive activity becomes more simple, less differentiated, so that other objects than the usual ones are able to release the action which, in cases of a less strong drive, would be released by the normal object alone. The actions released by such inadequate objects are sometimes called *"substitutive"* or *"symbolic"* actions. Birds may then be observed to brood on stones instead of their eggs, hungry animals to eat things that are not suited for their food. Many cases quoted before as examples of an inappropriate functioning of instinct through errors of perception may be regarded as examples of such substitutive actions as well. A strong inner drive, then, requires so little outer stimulus for releasing an instinctive activity that this activity in many cases becomes sterile. Some investigators even go so far as to believe that under the urge of a very strong drive instinctive actions may be executed without any outer perception at all ("Leerlaufreaktionen" of Lorenz). The examples quoted to show this, however, are not wholly convincing : it is not always easy to prove that an animal really does not perceive anything at all at such a moment. Anyhow it is certain that under a strong inner drive perceptions but little differentiated may be able to release the whole chain of instinctive activity.

A greater number of instincts, however, are released by *cognitions of outer origin*, be these simple sensations or more or less complex perceptions. But in many of these cases inner cognitions also play a rôle. It is only in a state of hunger, when experiencing the bodily sensation of an empty stomach and the discomfort caused by it, that the beast of prey attacks its victim ; it is only when it is in heat that the male behaves in a special way at the perception of a congener of the other or the same sex. In such cases, therefore, an instinct may be said to be of mixed origin. But in such cases the rôle of outer cognitions is so much more decisive for the execution of the action than that of the inner sensations, that we may regard the latter simply as the conditions necessary for releasing and full functioning of the instinct on outer perceptions, and therefore for the present we may pass over them here.

Now, these outer cognitions may be simple *sensations*, or more or less complex *perceptions*. Let us begin with the instincts evoked by simple sensations, such as those of light, gravity, heat, moisture, etc. These instincts may be divided into two classes, according to whether the instinctive action is, or is not, directed with regard to the location of the source of stimulation. In the former case we speak of *orientating-instincts*, in the latter of *alarming-instincts*. Let us first say some words about these alarming-instincts.

Many animals show the peculiarity that sudden sensations evoke in them a typical self-protecting behaviour. Animals that live in tubes or other protecting coverings contract, when stimulated by light, or by shadow, or by both of these. So the tube-worm Serpula uncinata contracts in its tube when a shadow falls on it, while it does not react to a ray of light ;

snails, like Helix or Limnaea, in this case retract their antennæ, Pecten closes its shell, etc. Other animals only react to light, as for instance the Ascidian Ciona intestinalis. Some mussels, such as Mya arenaria, react to light as well as to shadow ; in the former case by contraction of the sipho, in the latter by contraction of its tentacles. Even the tortoise Testudo ibera draws its head in under its shell if a shadow strikes it, but does this also at the perception of a moving object in its neighbourhood, even if this does not throw a shadow on it. Here the same reaction may be evoked by a simple sensation as well as by more complex perception.[1]

Other sensations, too, may evoke similar actions. Sensations of touch have the same effect on sea-anemones and tube-worms : they retire under the sand or contract their tube. The tube-worm Spirographis spallanzanii according to Winterstein retires into its tube if, at a short distance from it, an organ-pipe is blown in the water. Hydra, according to Mast, contracts if a capillary tube with hot or cold water is placed near to its neighbourhood. All these actions are to be understood as actions of flight or self-protection at the perception of menacing danger.

In other cases such alarming sensations may have a stimulating effect on the animal. This is especially the case with sensations of light. If the little Medusa Gonionemus is struck by a ray of light, according to Yerkes, it begins to move and swim round till by chance it comes into a shaded part of the aquarium, where it comes to rest. The result of this is that after some time all the animals find themselves in the darker part of the aquarium. This flocking together in the dark must be carefully distinguished from the directed movements towards the dark which we shall soon have to speak of. A similar alarm by light may be observed in many other animals. That this is more than a simple physiological stimulation by the light is shown by the fact that Asterias forreri, according to Jennings, if struck by a strong light,

---

[1] Physiologists are inclined to call these reactions light- or shadow-"reflexes.' For reasons stated in the former chapter we cannot adopt this terminology, but regard them as innate actions of the animal as a whole, directed to personal self-protection.

becomes restless and creeps about until it comes to a place where the intensity of the light is less. Should the animal be engaged in eating at the moment of the illumination, it leaves its food and creeps away. The sensation of strong light, therefore, apparently evokes a feeling of discomfort or pain in the animal ; otherwise it would certainly not have stopped eating and, if it had been a question of physiological stimulation alone, probably would have started to eat faster than before.

Other sensations also may induce flight-reactions of this kind. We have already seen that Hydra contracts when a tube with hot water at about 60° is brought near to it. With water of a still higher temperature the animals loosen themselves from the soil and swim away, but the direction of this swimming, according to Mast, shows no relation to that of the stimulation. The woodlouse Porcellio scaber, according to Gunn, becomes active when the humidity of the air diminishes ; with the grasshopper Locusta migratoria, according to Kennedy, the contrary is the case, the animal becoming active when the humidity of the air increases, while it comes to rest when the air grows drier. For those who know the biological needs of these animals the purposefulness of these instinctive flight actions is not difficult to understand.

Physiologists are inclined to regard all these activities of animals under the influence of light sensations as the effect of purely physiological stimulation. But the case of the starfish leaving its food when struck by light has already led us to understand that there is more in these reactions than a simple physiological phenomenon. This is shown still more clearly in a case described by Hovey with the marine flat-worm Leptoplana. This animal shows a strong reaction to light, and starts moving at a sudden light-sensation, caused when the stone under which it is hiding is turned over. On the other hand it shows a negative reaction and withdraws for a short distance when its head is touched. Hovey now succeeded in partly breaking the animals of their light reaction by touching their head every time they moved as the result of a sudden illumination. In control experiments it was shown that neither adaptation to light, nor tiredness, or any injury to the head of the worms, was the cause of the change of their behaviour. The experience acquired by the animal, namely, that illumination was a signal for a subsequent touch on its head, induced it more or less to change its innate reaction to the light. The psychological element of experience, to which we shall return in a following chapter, therefore interferes in the innate reaction of flight from strong light. In this respect these alarming-instincts do not differ from the higher instincts we shall presently have to describe.

More important, however, than these instincts in which animals are merely alarmed by special sensations are those in which such sensations induce animals to move in a direction related to that of the source of stimulation. These *orientating-instincts* are known as " *tropisms*," " *taxes* " or " *tactic movements*."

First a few words as to these terms. The term "tropism" was introduced by the old botanists for the description of the curving of growing plants under the influence of light. When later the movements of free-moving organisms, or plant-spores, towards, or away from, the light were discovered, these at first were also called tropisms. Later on a distinction was made between "tropisms," such as the curving of fixed plants, and "taxes" or "tactic movements" such as the movements of free-moving organisms towards, or away from, a source of stimulation. It is advisable to adopt this distinction. There are only a few cases of such tropisms in the animal world ; thus, growing polyps of Hydrozoa, according to Loeb, grow out in the direction of the light. This directed growth, however, is probably caused simply by an unequal growth at the illuminated, and the non-illuminated side of the polyp, and there would seem to be no reason to admit that any psychical element is involved in it. So we may leave these phenomena and the study of them to the physiologist.

There remain, then, the taxes and tactic movements. It seems profitable here to make a distinction similar to that we made before between instincts and instinctive actions. Taxes, then, are the inner factors, responsible for the directed movements towards, or from, a source of stimulation ; these movements themselves we call tactic movements.

Among these tactic movements we may again distinguish two main classes. The first one bears the name of *"phobo-taxis,"* the second one that of *"topotaxis."* These names were invented by the botanist Pfeffer, and afterwards adopted by Kühn in his pioneering work on the orientation of animals in space. The term "phobotaxis" has undergone some criticism of later years ; it indeed suggests something not quite defensible, namely, the fact that something like fear (the Greek "phobos") lies at the bottom of these reactions. We, of course, do not know very much about the feelings of animals, especially of the lower ones, but it does not seem very probable that anything like a real feeling of fear would induce a Protozoan to react in a special way to light stimulation. In the term "topotaxis," on the other hand, nothing is suggested about a concomitant feeling. But as it is not wise to change technical terms that have become current, we will continue to speak of phobotaxis as well as of topotaxis.

It is not necessary in this work to go very deeply into the difference between phobotaxes and topotaxes. There is a difference on the side of cognition that must be ascribed to a difference in the structure of the respective sense organs of the animals : phobotaxes are evoked by a sensation of difference in stimulation between two succeeding stimuli ; in topotaxis on the other hand there is a sensation of difference in stimulation between two simultaneous stimuli. Connected with these differences in the cognition there are differences in the movements that are caused by them : in phobotaxes the movements are not directly orientated with regard to the direction of the stimulus, while in topotaxes the movements are so orientated. But the final result is the same : either directly or indirectly the animal moves towards, or away from, the source of stimulation, in phobotaxis as well as in topotaxis. For the rest, phobic and topic orientation may alternate in the same animal ; many animals react in a phobic way at some distance from the source of stimulation, while nearer to it they react in a topic way, and in many cases the reaction is such that it cannot definitely be said if we have to do with a phobo- or a topotaxis. From the psychological point of view the differences between the two groups are not very essential.

We may therefore here disregard these differences and consider what the two classes of taxes have in common. This common character is that their movements are directed towards, or away from, a source of stimulation. This stimulation may be caused by a ray of light, by the pressure of gravity, by the heat from a warm spot. If the movement is directed towards the stimulus we speak of a positive taxis ; if directed away from it of a negative one. Sometimes also the animal orientates itself transversely, or obliquely, with respect to the stimulus. We may, however, disregard this form here.

The best-known cases of such taxes are found where animals react to a stimulation by light. These phenomena are called "phototaxes." Most of the lower animals that have organs capable of perceiving either the intensity or the direction of a ray of light, show a positive or negative phototaxis. If a pseudopodium of a forward-moving Amoeba is struck by a ray of light, the forward movement is stopped, the pseudopodium retracted and a new one formed at another place. If this new pseudopodium again reaches the light spot, it is again retracted and a new one formed, and so on, till finally a pseudopodium is formed that is no longer touched by the light. Then the whole body of the Amoeba follows this new pseudopodium, and the animal creeps away from the light. Here the sensation of a difference in successive light stimulations is followed by a movement that indirectly leads the animal away from the light, a good example therefore of phobotaxis. Similar phobic reactions towards, or from, the light may be observed in many swimming Protozoa, although executed in a somewhat different way.

Another case is found with animals that possess eyes capable of the perception of the direction of light. If the young larvæ of the Polychæte worm Arenicola cristata is affected on one side by the light, the animal, according to Mast, at once turns sharply towards it. The contrary is shown by animals like the flat-worm Planaria maculata, which immediately turn away if a ray of light falls on them. Here we have examples of topotactic reactions, the former positive, the latter negative.

It is especially in insects and their larvæ that many examples of such light reactions are to be found. It is not possible to give a definite rule about the sign of the taxis ; this often changes with the age or the state of the animal, while hunger and sexual maturation may also influence the direction of the movement. Further, the sign of the taxis often changes with the intensity of the stimulus : animals that are positive to weak light react negatively in strong light. It is not difficult to find a parallel to these changes in the instinctive life of higher animals : if a small enemy is met with, the instinct of attack prevails, while if the enemy is big and strong the instinct of self-protection may prevail, and the animal seeks safety in flight. For the rest, in the higher animals movements released by such simple light sensations are rare ; their place is taken by actions released by more complex perceptions, although phototaxis may be found in the larvæ of fishes and in young mammals before the eyes are open.

Similar tactic movements are to be found as reactions to other sensations as well. "Geotaxes" are movements upwards or downwards, against, or in the direction of, gravity, according as the geotaxis is negative or positive. If Medusæ are disturbed, they swim to the surface of the water in a negative geotaxis ; on a strong illumination, on the contrary, they swim, in positive geotaxis, downwards to the bottom of the aquarium. In "hygrotaxis" the animal strives to go to, or away from, the water or a moist place. When Savory studied the behaviour of two species of spiders, Zilla-X-notata and Zilla atrica in a basin with water on one side and dry on the other side, he found that while the former species always went to the dry side, the latter looked for a place near the water. In "thermotaxis" we find a flight from extreme temperatures and an endeavour to find an optimal temperature, different for each species. "Rheotaxis" brings Planaria or fishes to react to the direction of the stream of water, whether by these movements it is prevented from being carried away by the stream, or whether by creeping against the stream it reaches places where food is more abundant. In the same way we speak of "anemotaxis" when animals sit with their heads directed towards, or away from, the wind. The sensation of touch may evoke positive or negative "thigmotactic" reactions : sometimes animals in a positive thigmotaxis try to keep in contact with a fixed body, like a stone, or stay in a fissure or hole ; in other cases they contract, or turn aside, in negative thigmotaxis if suddenly touched by a moving object. Finally, we speak of "vibrotaxis" if animals react to the sensation of vibrations in their neighbourhood. The best-known instance of such a positive vibrotaxis is the reaction of the spider, if some insect has flown into its web.

Whether we may rightly speak of "chemotaxis" in the strict sense of the word is doubtful. Of course there are many positive or negative reactions to chemical stimulations in animals, but as a rule these stimuli are too complex to be regarded as arousing simple sensations. It is not the sensation of smell in general, but a special smell-perception that causes the animal to follow its prey or to seek for its sex-partner, the propinquity of which it has discovered by smell. These chemical reactions form a transition between taxes in the strict sense of the word and the more complex forms of instincts, which we shall soon have to consider.

Now, what all these taxes have in common is that a sensation of some kind has the effect of making the animal move in a direction that stands in a certain relation to that of the source of the stimulation. For one who knows the vital wants of an animal at a special period of its life, it is not difficult to understand the purposefulness of these movements. If water is saturated with carbon dioxide, swimming towards the light in normal circumstances brings the water-flea Daphnia into regions where there is more oxygen, and a similar effect is reached by the negative geotaxis, shown by Paramæcium, if numbers of them are together in a small tube or if the carbon dioxide tension of the water is heightened. While tadpoles and young fishes in general are indifferent to light, they may be made positively phototactic if brought together in greater numbers in a small glass.

Thus, Franz found that if 15 tadpoles were put together into a glass of 4.7 cm. diameter with 5 cm. height of water, the animals swam round in all directions. If, on the contrary, he put them into a similar glass with 1.5 cm. water, they suddenly showed a marked positive phototaxis and swam to the light. Phototaxis in this case must be regarded as an instinctive flight reaction, evoked by the constant contact with the other tadpoles. Koehler, at least, found that a similar phototaxis may be aroused in tadpoles swimming in small numbers in fresh water, if they are gently touched with a brush. It is a well-known fact that flies in a room, when suddenly roused, fly to the windows in positive phototaxis in an effort to escape. Positive thermotaxis brings parasites of warm-blooded animals to their hosts ; positive rheotaxis, as we saw already, has the effect that fish in a stream remain at about the same place, thus preventing their being washed down by the current, although in many cases this effect is reached more by visual perception of the apparent movement of the banks than by the sensation of the flow of the water. So all tactic movements, aroused in the laboratory by various stimulations, may be regarded as instinctive actions, being under natural conditions directed towards the preservation of life or the flight from danger.

Now these simple instincts or taxes may, like the more complex instincts, in some cases be changed by the influence of acquired experience. We have already seen that Hovev partly succeeded in breaking Leptoplana of its photokinesis. In a similar way Blees succeeded in temporarily breaking the positive phototaxis in Daphnia. To this end he placed positively phototactic Daphnias in a bent tube, one arm of which stood vertically in the water, while the other arm, 10 cm. long, was kept horizontal. The animals were inserted with a pipette to the point where the horizontal arm began. At first this horizontal arm was directed towards the light ; the animals then immediately swam through it to the light. Then the horizontal arm was turned somewhat way from the light, first 45°, then 90°. The animals had now to learn that they had first to swim obliquely or transversely to the light through this horizontal arm of the tube, and only after having

6

left it could they swim straight in the direction of the light. This learning was measured by the number of times they struck against the wall at the light side of the tube and by the time they needed to pass through the horizontal arm. After they had learned to do so, the horizontal arm was turned 135° and finally even 180° away from the light. The animals were now able, first to swim away from the light in the horizontal arm and then to move towards the light as soon as they found the way free. In learning this, the number of times they touched the wall of the tube and the time they required for the passage through it lessened. Thus, when the horizontal arm was turned away 135° from the light, the averages for three successive experiments with four animals on one day went down from 87 to 78 and 45 touches and from 425 to 325 and 235 seconds respectively. When the arm was turned straight away from the light, the averages of three experiments with two animals on one day were 39, 19, and 13 touches and 110, 48, and 30 seconds respectively. Untrained animals were not able to do this : four of them remained for 15 minutes at the bend of the tube and could not be brought to swim against the light. It is clear that this change in the behaviour of the trained animals must be ascribed to experience. This experience was that to give up the tendency to swim to the light for some moments would bring them to a point from where swimming towards the light would again be possible. True, this experience is assuredly not so explicit as we here describe it, a point to which we will come back in a following chapter. But of whatever nature it may be, this influence of acquired experience on innate behaviour points to a psychical element underlying this behaviour itself. Taxes are not simple physiological phenomena, as some physiologists assert. They are the expressions of psychical phenomena in animals, just as the higher instincts are.

For the rest, there are several intermediate cases between taxes and these higher instincts, between instincts evoked by simple sensations and those evoked by real perceptions. We have already seen that it is doubtful whether we may speak of real chemotaxis. That is, the positive or negative reactions to chemical stimuli are mostly evoked not by a simple chemical sensation, by the sensation of some chemical stimulus as such, but by a definite chemical perception, such as the smell of food or the scent of an enemy. In the visual sphere, too, simple perceptions may often evoke instinctive actions. As a first instance of these we may quote the cases of so-called "scototaxes." We have seen that many animals are negatively phototactic, i.e., they go away from the light. On the other hand, if black screens are placed in the field, some animals react positively to these screens and try to reach them. This was formerly regarded as a case of negative phototaxis, but later it has been shown that it is distinct from this. It is a positive reaction to the perception of a dark screen (and for this reason the term "taxis" here is not altogether correct), whereas, in the former case, there was a negative reaction to a simple sensation. We saw further that the sensation of shadow or light induces tube-worms to contract. The same effect may be reached with Testudo, if it perceives a moving object in its neighbourhood. The mussel Pecten is alarmed by the perception of the movement of its enemy, the starfish Asterias, but also, as von Uexküll observed, by the slow moving of a hand with open fingers along the wall of the aquarium. Another case of such instincts evoked by simple perception has been described by Mast of the firefly Photinus pyralis. The males of this beetle fly round in the dark, and send out a flash of light about every five seconds. The females sit in the grass and react to the perception of these flashes with their own flashes of light, of lesser intensity and of longer duration than those of the males. The males then turn towards the females until, after repeated flashes, the animals find each other and copulate. The males know how to distinguish between the flashes of their own sex and those of the females, and still turn towards the latter after their flashing is finished. The points of agreement and difference between these phenomena and positive phototaxes will be clear : it is a perception of light, not, however, of light in general, but of a special form of light emission, that evokes the approaching of the males.

We have already seen that the perceptions that release

instinctive actions are in many cases much more simple than was formerly admitted and that just this simplicity is the cause why so often animals are led astray and commit errors, sometimes fatal to themselves. It is necessary, therefore, to distinguish between the apparent and the real releasing perception in instincts. A closer analysis of this releasing perception will certainly show us many more examples of their simplicity. Of recent years much good analytical work in this line has been done. All this again proves that there are only gradual transitions between taxes and the higher instincts, and that it could be wrong to regard taxes as phenomena of a nature essentially different from that of instincts.

The reader will not expect us here to give a survey of all these higher instincts in animals, higher in so far as they are evoked by more or less complex perceptions and not by simple sensations, higher also in so far as their actions are not simple movements, but form a more or less complicated behaviour. This field is so immense and the instinctive actions of animals are so innumerable that it would fill many larger volumes than this to enumerate them. For the rest we have already described a number of them in our general considerations about the nature of instinct. Let us conclude this section by describing one more example of such higher instincts, a case that may be regarded as a standard example, in so far as several characters of instinct, e.g., its innateness, its purposefulness, the fact that the action is performed without being understood by the animal, the correlation between instinct and morphological structure, etc., stand out clearly. This, then, is the instinct of the care for the brood in the Yucca-moth, as it was first described by Riley some sixty years ago.

The Yucca-moth, Pronuba yuccasella, is a small moth, the imagines of which come out of the pupa at the same time as the flowers of the Yucca-plant (Yucca filamentosa) open for a few nights. Males and females of the moth find each other and copulate ; then the female flies to an open flower of the Yucca, takes some pollen from the stamina of it and kneads it into a ball with the help of her great sickle-shaped maxillary tentacles. She then carries the collected pollen away to another Yucca-flower. There, with the aid of her sharp ovipositor, she opens the ovary of the flower and deposits her eggs between the ovules of the plant ; then she climbs upwards along the style to the stigma, and presses the pollen she brought with her into the opening of it. Herewith she achieves the fertilisation of the plant, which without her help probably would not have occurred, as this moth is one of the few insects, or the only one, that pollinates Yuccas. Through this complicated behaviour, however, the moth achieves the propagation of her own species as well as that of the plant, as her growing larvæ feed only on the developing ovules of the Yucca and would therefore perish if these ovules were not brought to development. And as, on the other hand, so large a number of ovules of the plant are fertilised that only a part of them will serve as food to the larvæ, both the plant and the moth have to thank this instinctive behaviour of the moth for their propagation.

These actions of the moth indeed bear all the marks of instinctive behaviour. They are innate : no other moth has served as an example to the animal when performing its actions. The moth does not know, cannot know, the end towards which her behaviour is directed. That she has no idea about the necessity or desirability of the continuance of the life of her species, not to speak of that of the plant, is obvious. The behaviour is characteristic of the species ; all Yucca-moths behave in the same way. It is purposive, in this case not only for the species of the moth but, curiously enough, also for that of another living being, the plant. Interesting, further, are the morphological adaptations of the moth to her work ; she is the only moth with an ovipositor, and the only one that possesses the great sickle-shaped maxillary tentacles which enable her to knead and to carry away the pollen. What outer perceptions exactly release the different parts of her behaviour has not yet been determined. Whether, for instance, she is attracted by the smell or the sight of the white flowers is not known, nor if some negative geotaxis plays a rôle in her climbing the style after having laid her eggs. As to the inner sensation, we may safely assume that the sensation of the ripe and fertilised eggs in her body provide the inner condition for the seeking of a flower.

With this example of a highly specialised and complex instinct of an insect we may conclude the description of animal instincts. We did not end with this one for the reason that animal instincts are not found above the insect level. As we saw already, instincts and instinctive tendencies are to be found in the higher animals as well. With them, however, they lose their narrower specialised character, so that even careful students of the life of higher animals are sometimes apt to overlook them. But it would be wrong to suppose that the instincts are not there. The whole behaviour of animals is based on the foundation of their instincts. As we will see in a later chapter, such actions of theirs as deserve to be called intelligent issue from their instinctive activity ; their intelligence is built up on their instinct. Instincts are the kernel of all animal behaviour, be it simply innate, or guided by intelligence.

We quoted at the beginning of this chapter as a provisional definition of instinct, that of Romanes, pronounced some sixty years ago. Since then our knowledge concerning the essence of instinct has been considerably increased. Are we now, at the end of this chapter, in a position to give a more definite, and perhaps more analytical, definition ?

With this in view we must bear in mind that an instinct is released by a cognition, the nature of which we have discussed above. We also know that an instinct ends in a striving, a conation, that impels to some activity, till an end is reached, the perception of which makes the animal cease its action. But is this all that happens within the animal, or is there one more link in the chain uniting the conation to the cognition ?

Let us consider the case of some higher animal, for instance, of the hare that sees or hears the hounds, and flies for its life. Or, rather, let us first consider that of a man in similar circumstances, a man who has committed some crime and now becomes aware that the police are at his heels. In such a case the criminal behaves like a startled animal, and flies for his life, till some safe place is reached. But we know that in this case there is one more inner experience between the perception and the striving, namely, the feeling of fear, evoked by the perception of the approaching police. No one will deny that a similar feeling of fear must be experienced by the hare when pursued by the hounds : the scudding animal clearly bears all the signs of it. The truth is, therefore, that the perception of the pursuing enemy evokes the feeling of fear, and the feeling of fear in its turn evokes the desire to escape and the striving to get away from the danger, which causes the animal to fly, till a place is reached which evokes a feeling of security that brings the flight to a stop. In other words, between the cognition and the conation there is some experience that links them together, namely, an affection of some kind. In a similar way another affection, say, a feeling of satisfaction at the perception of the goal reached, brings the conation to an end. The same is the case with other instincts. The perception of the grain would not induce the chicken to pick it up were it not moved by some feeling of appetence ; the female could not induce the male in heat to try to copulate with her without some feeling of lust evoked in him by the perception of the female. The same must be the case with lower animals, although the feelings of lower animals are certainly so very different from ours that it is difficult, if not impossible, to describe them adequately in terms of human experiences. But some feeling must lead the wasp to paralyse the caterpillar it has discovered and the termites in the nest to attend to the queen. We have already seen that with bodily sensations, like those of hunger or thirst, it is a feeling of pain or discomfort, caused by these sensations, that leads the animal to go round in search of the food or water. Some feeling of discomfort makes the Daphnia, in unclean water, fly towards the light. Even in Amoeba, floating freely in the water, as we saw in our first chapter, some feeling we shall not try to describe brings it to seek for a fixed object. Our inability to make any very definite statements about these feelings should not be a reason for us to ignore, or even to deny, them. When sailing on the sea we are not able to say very much that is definite about the animal life below our vessel ; yet it would be foolish and erroneous if for that reason we should wholly deny its existence.

These considerations bring us to a more profound and analytical definition of instinct than that of Romanes. *Instinct, then, is a linking, and indeed an innate and specific linking, between a cognition, an affection, and a conation.* But this linking does not confine itself to one direction only. Just as the perception instinctively calls forth the feeling, and the feeling the striving, so also inversely the striving influences the perception and the feeling of the animal. The perceptions of the animals are as dependent on their striving as their striving is on their perceptions ; the animal striving to have its hunger appeased perceives the prey that will serve as food, but probably scarcely perceives objects not suitable for this purpose. The male hare in heat will probably not notice the female mouse ; the hunting wolf will not perceive the branches of the tree so important for the bird seeking a place to build its nest. By its striving the objects in its world acquire for the animal a special meaning, a special "valence," as it has been called. The rabbit has no valence for the calf, nor the clover for the weasel. And in the same way the feelings of the animals are dependent on their striving : in a male in heat a male of his own species evokes the feeling of hostility, whereas it is an indifferent being to him if he is not stirred by his sexual instinct. To a dog gnawing a bone his playmate of a quarter of an hour ago becomes a rival and an enemy.

We may therefore conclude with the following *definition of an instinct.* Under instinct in animals we understand that characteristic innate psychic disposition, through which special sensations or perceptions, evoked by special stimuli, evoke themselves special feelings and emotions, and these in their turn evoke special drives and strivings, which express themselves in special actions, directed to a special goal ; while, on the other hand also, special perceptions and feelings are evoked and influenced by special strivings. Or, to put it more briefly : *Instinct is the innate psychological structure which couples a special affection to a special cognition and a special conation to a special affection, and on the other hand*

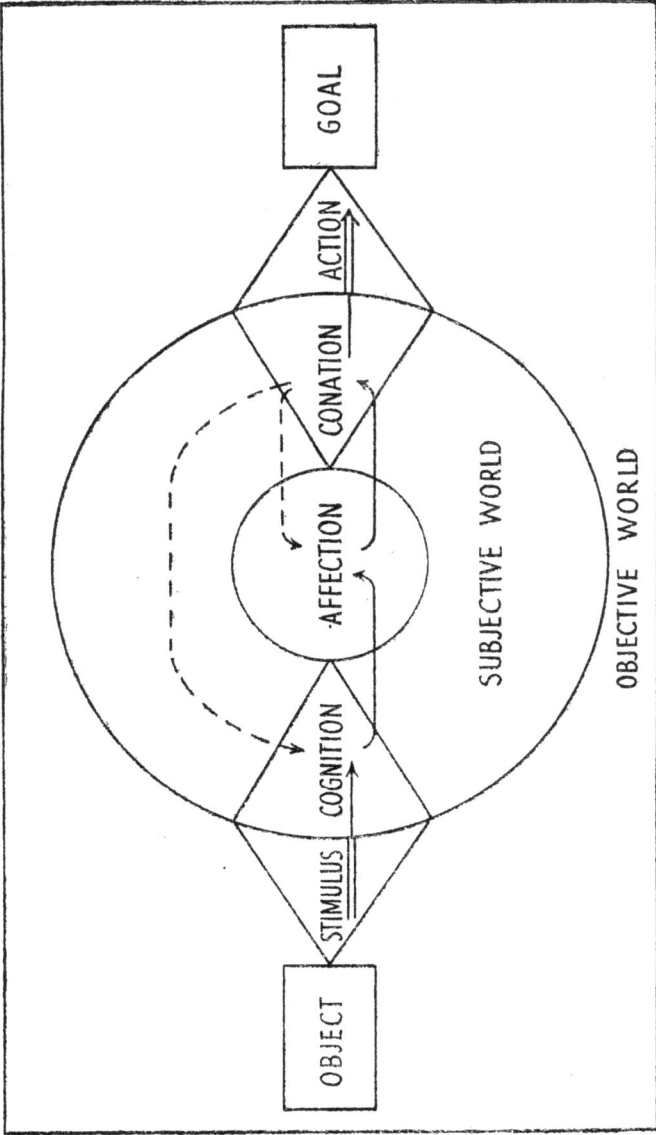

Diagram of Instinct

couples a special cognition and an affection to a special conation.
We have endeavoured to express this in the diagram on
the previous page (p. 89).

It will be remarked that this definition of instinct is *a
purely psychological one,* i.e. it contains only psychological
concepts, in contrast to many older definitions which con-
tained biological concepts like "purposefulness," "vital
needs," and the like. Instinct is a psychological phenomenon,
and must therefore be defined in psychological terms ; the
instinctive action is a biological phenomenon and may be
defined in terms of biology. But as we are writing on the
psychology of animals, the latter aspect holds no interest for
us for the moment.

CHAPTER III

THE PROBLEM OF ANIMAL LEARNING

I N the preceding chapter we have seen that instinctive
actions are innate and specific, i.e. that they have not to be
learnt by the animal, and are characteristic of the species to
which the animal belongs and not of the individual animal
itself. But it is the individual, and not the species, which
is the real living being, a being which grows and develops,
which perceives and feels, remembers and gathers experience.
And as a result of all this, the innate behaviour of an animal
may change during the course of its life.

All these changes in the innate behaviour we summarize
under the concept of "learning." Learning, then, taken in
the broadest sense of the word, may be defined as *that inner
process by which changes are introduced into the original
behaviour of an individual.* But we must at once add that not
all these changes have a psychological origin. Therefore we
must distinguish between learning based on physiological
and that based on psychological phenomena, and, although
strictly speaking the first form of learning falls beyond the

scope of this book, it would seem necessary, to avoid confusion, to say a few words on this physiological mode of learning too.

First, then, there is learning based on *physiological maturation*. The body of the young animal changes, it grows and develops. Its muscles become stronger, nerve connections grow and the innervation of special muscles becomes better than it was before. The result of this is that the execution of special movements improves. A good instance of this form of learning is that of the young bird learning to fly. That this learning in many cases is not the result of experience has been stated by Lorenz. Young wood-pigeons (Columba palumbus) leave the nest very early, before the flight-feathers are fully grown, whereas with the rock-dove (Columba livia) the young ones fly out later, when the wings are quite developed. Although the young rock-doves have no experience in flying and have had no room to practise, according to Lorenz they fly from the very start just as well as the young wˮˮd-pigeons which have been flying for some days. This is surely due to bodily maturation.

That this is so has been proved experimentally by Grohmann. He kept young pigeons in small boxes in which they could not turn round nor by any means open their wings. One of them was set free after it had been confined in such a box from the 12th to the 37th day of its life. The bird at once began to flutter, twelve minutes later flew from the floor on to a 25-cm. high box, after one hour flew up vertically to a height of half a metre and the next day flew as high and as well as a pigeon that had not been confined at all. Another bird, set free on the 55th day, at once flew away 40 metres on to a fence 1.80 m. in height. It was clear that the flying had not had to be learnt by experience or practice, but that the skill was the result of a physiological maturation. Similar results had indeed been obtained by Spalding some seventy years ago, with swallows, titmice, and wrens. Yet, as we soon shall see, these results must not be generalized.

Another change in behaviour, not attributable to a psychological factor, is that which is caused by *physiological fatigue or habituation of the sense organs.* If not too strong a stimulus be applied for some time to an animal, the animal gets habituated to the stimulus, and after some time changes its behaviour in so far as to react no longer to the stimulus in the same way as it originally did. There are a great number of cases known in the animal world of such a change in behaviour due to habituation. Thus Jennings found that Stentor and other Infusoria soon get habituated to a stream of water directed against them, and no longer contract. If Jennings let a drop of water fall from a height of 30 cm. on to the disc of the Anemone Aiptasia annulata, the animal at once contracted completely ; if, after the animal had again expanded, a second drop fell, the animal in many cases hardly reacted at all and the reaction wholly ceased after some further drops. Arbacia, according to Holmes, reacts on a shadowing by erecting its spines, but if this shadowing is repeated three or four times the animal stops doing it. This disappearance of the reaction sometimes stands in relation to the interval between the stimulations. Thus Hargitt observed that if a colony of the tube-worm Hydroides dianthus was shadowed by means of a swinging pendulum, so as to give a rhythmical shadowing at intervals of one second, all animals contracted at each shadowing, while at an interval of half a second a number of them reacted no longer after the first shadowings, and with intervals of a quarter of a second practically all the animals became indifferent to the shadowing after the first time. It will be clear that in all these cases it is not necessary to admit psychological experience as the cause of the change ; the phenomenon is based on a physiological habituation of the sense organs.

The reverse of this habituation to repeated stimulation may perhaps be found in cases in which the sensibility to a stimulus is raised by another previous stimulation. Sgonina found in Paramæcium that electrical stimulation lowers the threshold for optical stimuli and so causes a negative phototaxis in animals that before were indifferent to the light. If the conclusions he draws from these experiments are correct, we must admit that here again there is a change of behaviour on a physiological basis.

Less easy to analyse, and probably based on physiological as well as on psychological phenomena, is the *change of behaviour through practice*. When a billiard-player improves his play by practice, the change from his original more or less clumsy performance on the billiard-table is certainly for a great part based on the experience of former occasions when trying to hit the balls, not to speak of an element of reasoning and computation at the moment of striking. But if a child learns to walk, the improvement in its walking is not so much due to former experience, as to a better command over its movements caused by a better physiological functioning of necessary reflexes. In animals there are several instances of improvement in behaviour by practice, in which it is not easy to say whether it is effected in the way of the billiard-player or of the child. Kortlandt reports that young cormorants at first fly very awkwardly, but that after twenty hours of flying there is no longer any difference between their flying and that of adult birds. The fact that it takes rather a long time to reach this stage seems to prove that in this case physiological maturation alone is not responsible for this improvement, but that it must also be partly ascribed to practice. The same was found by Dennis with young buzzards. Unfledged birds, kept in boxes for ten weeks, after being set free, flew much worse than equally old birds not encaged. The cause of this difference can only be lack of practice. If this be so, the learning to fly must with these birds be of the same nature as that of the child learning to walk. If, on the other hand, a bird of prey by practice obtains skill in seizing its prey, there probably is also an element of experience in this improvement.

But more interesting to us are the cases in which learning is based on *psychological factors* alone. Here again we must distinguish between two possibilities : the learning may either be the result of a *psychical maturation*, or it is the result of *experience*. When a child is learning to speak, its learning for a large part is the result of psychical development : a backward child learns to speak only with great difficulty, no matter how much trouble its parents may take to hasten the process. The instances of deferred instincts, mentioned in our last chapter, may be regarded as cases of "learning" by psychological maturation, the word learning being taken in the broad sense as defined before. As an example of this we may refer to the development of the activity of the bees in the hive, as amply discussed in the preceding chapter.

The most important to us, however, are the cases in which the change of behaviour, in other words, the learning, is due to *acquired experience*. For here the behaviour of an animal reaches a higher level. Where former experience plays a rôle in the behaviour of an animal, we may say that this behaviour is no longer guided solely by instinct, but a new element has appeared on the scene, namely, *intelligence*. This intelligence in its different forms will be the subject of the discussions in the following chapters. It was only to preclude confusion that we thought it advisable, before proceeding, to say a few words on the different ways in which learning may be effected in the animal world, and to point to the difference between a non-intelligent and an intelligent way of learning.

CHAPTER IV

THE PROBLEM OF ANIMAL INTELLIGENCE

I F, now, we are to discuss in this chapter the problem of animal intelligence, it will be well to ask ourselves first, what this idea of intelligence may mean in the field of animal psychology.

The answer to this question is not at once clear. The concept "intelligence," it will be realized, is borrowed from human psychology. Now, in man, intelligence is not a simple function of the mind ; the concept of intelligence, therefore, is for the human psychologist not so simple and clear as is the concept of "heart" for the anatomist, or that of "blood-circulation" for the physiologist. "Intelligence" embraces in man a number of collaborating and interlocking psychical functions, like those of attention and memory, of imagination and ideation, of reason and judgment and the like, which, all together, influence and improve his original innate behaviour. In human psychology, therefore, the word intelligence is often used in rather different senses, according as the accent is laid on one or another of these functions, so much so that Spearman even goes so far as to doubt if the word has yet any scientific meaning at all. As a rule it is restricted to denoting a function of practical life, while the word "reasoning" or "intellect" is reserved for the capacity for conceptual thinking. Intelligence, then, is the capacity to deal adequately with new and unexpected circumstances, the capacity in such circumstances to grasp the essential in an object or situation, and to use this insight to reach a desired end. But, as we said, there is no general agreement in this matter.

With the animals the case is somewhat different and up to a certain point, more simple. Some of the functions mentioned above are not to be found in animals, or are to be found only in such an embryonic degree of development that we may ignore them. Many animals, and certainly the higher orders, exhibit the phenomenon of attention, and even among the lower orders many animals show memory. But do animals show imagination, and do they have free ideas ? One may doubt it. Anyhow, the faculty of abstraction certainly fails them. So with the animals the concept of intelligence may have a more restricted meaning than in man. With them we may relinquish its abstract aspects and use the word in its practical sense alone. But, on the other hand, if with the animals we try to apply the above-mentioned definition of "grasping the essential in an object or situation," and the "using this to reach a desired end," that we found useful in the case of man, we encounter the facts of instinct and instinctive activity.

Let us consider once more the case of the Yucca-moth, fertilising the Yucca-plant, or that of a fossorial wasp, paralysing her prey and dragging it into her hole as a food for her future offspring, or even the simple case of the young mammal, sucking at his mother's teats to appease his hunger. We certainly encounter in these animals a grasping of the essentials of the parts of the plant or of the body of the caterpillar or the breast of the mother, and the using of them as means to reach their particular biological end. Yet in these cases there is no reason to speak of intelligence. If, as we saw to be the case in instinctive activity, the end is not explicitly known, there can be no question of intelligence in the sense defined above of apprehending and using the essentials of a situation to attain a psychologically desired end. At best we might speak of an "implicit intelligence," if this expression has any meaning at all. The above-mentioned definition of intelligence, therefore, fails us in the case of animals.

With animals, therefore, we must approach the subject from another side. We have seen that all their activity is stirred by instincts, instincts that are inborn and not acquired, and are typical for the species and not for the individual, so that originally all animals of the same species may be expected to act in a similar way under similar circumstances (provided for a moment we pass over such slight differences as are caused by the normal variation in instincts). If, then, in animals we wish to distinguish intelligent actions, actions that bear the mark of intelligence, from these instinctive ones, we must lay stress on such characteristics of animal activity as deviate from those of their instinctive behaviour. We then observe that much of animal behaviour is acquired and not innate, that therefore it is characteristic of the individual and not of the species. This behaviour, then, we will call "intelligent." If one agrees with this or, perhaps better, if this distinction between intelligent and instinctive activity in animals be accepted as being the only way to obtain a clear distinction between the two and to outline them sharply, one will agree with the view which defines intelligence as *"the faculty to improve upon inborn instinctive actions in the light of past experience,"* or, better perhaps, *"to rebuild innate instincts in the light of such experience."* It will be clear that this definition is wider than that given above for human intelligence, and is based on another aspect of intelligence *qua* general phenomenon. But it will also be clear that this is the most helpful definition if, in animals, we wish to distinguish between instinctive and intelligent activity.

It will be understood, now, that this profiting by past experience so as to improve upon innate behaviour presupposes two other faculties of the animal mind. The first of these is that the animal must be able consciously to notice and to experience its own actions and their consequences to itself ; the second one is that it must be able to retain these experiences for a longer or shorter time. The first fact is connected with the psychological level on which the animal lives. An animal like a dog or a bird experiences much more than does a worm or a snail ; it has therefore more opportunity to let this experience influence its later actions. The retaining of this experience, then, is the function of its memory. Many researches have been made on memory in animals, about the duration of their retention, its different modalities, and so on. We cannot enter into all these questions, which stand only in indirect relation to the question which concerns us here. But we must not fail to take into account that it is not necessary to admit that what is experienced is also *explicitly* kept in the animal's mind, that, in other words, it is not necessary to believe that the animal later explicitly remembers : "When I was in these circumstances before, I did so or so, with such or such consequences for me." Doubtless the process as a rule occurs on the lower level of implicit remembrance. That is to say, the action or the result of an action evokes in the animal a certain feeling, be it one of pleasure in the case of an agreeable issue, or one of pain or discomfort if the action had a disagreeable effect. Now this positive or negative feeling overflows on to, and effectively colours, the action which evoked the feeling, so that the action itself becomes attractive or unattractive to the animal. This feeling may even colour the object or perception which released the original action, so that this object is invested with a special agreeable or disagreeable feeling. The champagne we have learned to drink at feasts afterwards "looks festive" ; the draught we tasted "looks nauseous." The perception, then, is infiltrated with the pleasant or unpleasant experience of the action released by it, or, to use an expression of Hobhouse, the feeling aroused by the releasing perception has assimilated the character of another feeling, which had followed it previously. If this process is repeated several times and the experience gained is strengthened by repetition, the original action in the one case will be executed directly and with pleasure, in the other case hesitatingly or not at all. Then the animal has changed its inborn behaviour in the light of past experience ; *it has shown intelligence*.

We may express this also in another way. In our second chapter we stated that if the perception of some object or situation instinctively evokes some action from the side of the animal, this object may be said to possess some innate meaning, some innate "valence" for the animal. The cat, whether perceived by hearing or by smell, has for the mouse the innate meaning of danger, and releases the affect of fear and the instinct of flight. Now an object or situation which originally did evoke a certain instinct, in other words, which had a special innate valence for an animal, by experience may acquire another valence and release another instinct, or perhaps may lose its original valence and no more evoke any instinct at all. In the same way an originally valence-less object may by experience acquire one, and so release some instinctive activity. We may consider these to be cases of *"re-valentiating"* and *"de-valentiating,"* and in the last mentioned case speak of *"valentiating"* objects by experience. All this new valentiating, all this change of valence, is the work of intelligence.

A simple example may make all this clear. A young dog meets for the first time in his life some animal unknown to him. Then this animal releases his instinct of curiosity, better perhaps, his instinct of examination. Suppose now this animal to be a cat, which herself reacts in an instinctive way towards the approaching dog. If the dog is big and the cat young and small, the perception of the dog will instinctively evoke fear in the cat and release her instinct of flight. This reaction of the cat stirs the hunting instinct of the dog and imparts to the animal "cat" the new valence of a prey to be hunted. But if the cat is strong and valorous she will not turn to flee at the sight of the dog but will defend herself, in a way perhaps which induces fear in the dog, causes him to stop in his examination, and releases his instinct of flight. The animal which originally had the valence of something to be examined may thus by experience acquire the valence of something to be hunted or to be feared.

An object without any valence may in the same way acquire a valence by experience. We have already seen an example of this in the behaviour of Paramæcium in Bramstedt's experiments. Paramæcium, which originally is indifferent to light, for which originally light has no valence, may learn to evade the lighter side of a drop of water if it has learnt by experience that this light involves a high temperature. The originally valenceless light herewith acquires the valence of something to be avoided.

It will be clear now that the breadth of instincts, of which we spoke in a former chapter, is of great importance for the acquiring of such experience, leading to the acquiring of a new valence, and therefore for the entrance of intelligence into the activity of an animal. If the instincts were absolutely rigid, if they had no breadth at all, so that only one particular perception is able to evoke one particular action, the possibility of acquiring experience would be very much limited. In the best case the animal would only learn to desist from such an innate action, if this action had unpleasant effects for it, supposing the drive to be not so strong that the animal cannot suppress it. If, on the other hand, an animal instinctively reacts to a number of kindred perceptions in a number of different ways, there is more occasion for it to experience that one reaction will have a more agreeable result for itself than another. The tern, which we saw has a narrow feeding-instinct and is specialized for catching its food by diving into the water, has much less opportunity to obtain experience of different kinds of food and different ways of obtaining it than the gull, which is an all-eater and catches its food in different ways. If in the case of the dog the only possible reaction of his examination-instinct was that of running at high speed straight towards every unknown object, there would be little occasion for him to gain experience as to the way to treat such strange things. Actually he may now run fast, now walk slowly, or even creep towards it, may walk prudently around it, may bark at it, may lie down and wait till the object moves, etc., according to whether the object is big or small, moves towards him or lies still. This variety of action gives him great opportunity to acquire experience, a very important thing, especially for an animal living in nature with all its threatening dangers.

Now, as a rule such experience is gathered from the casual happenings of daily life. But these happenings may be influenced in two ways. First man may occupy himself with an animal and thrust some special experience upon it. This process is called the "training" of an animal. By agreeable and disagreeable experience (food or caresses in one case, punishment or scolding on the other) the master trains his dog to do what he wants him to do : to follow him at his heels in the street, or to stay in his basket during dinner. In the same way, in the laboratory, the monkeys or fish, whose sense perceptions are being studied, are brought to learn by experience that if they choose a box or an opening with a special mark this means food, whereas choosing another one means an electric shock or some other kind of punishment. More important to the animal, however, than this human training is the influence of the conduct of any other animals with whom he is living in a social bond. By imitating the acts of its parents or other older congeners (which occurs especially where an individual with less initiative lives in a social bond with a more enterprising congener, as is the case with a young animal living together with older ones), by following their example and doing what it sees them doing and omitting what it sees them avoiding, the animal obtains a store of useful experience more rapidly than if it had been living alone. Morgan has reported several observations on the effect of this imitation. If the hen begins to pick, the chickens follow her example ; they pick at what they see other chickens picking at. If one chicken begins to drink from a dish, the others soon follow. According to Lorenz, the flight-reaction of young jackdaws is not at first released by the perception of a dangerous animal as such, but by the sight of the frightened parents. If this has happened several times the younger ones are frightened by the dangerous animal itself. Jackdaws that are reared by man therefore do not know danger, and the young of tame parents remain tame. Imitation therefore accelerates the process of obtaining experience.

Before ending these general remarks on animal intelligence we must point to three further aspects of it that are of importance to the animal. The first one is, that by experience an originally blind drive may be changed into a more or less conscious striving. The young animal which originally, without knowing why, makes sucking movements on the teats of its mother, learns by experience that these movements serve to appease its hunger. If, then, later it is hungry, it will probably seek the teats with the explicit knowledge of the end it wishes to reach. The young bird may the first time sit upon its eggs without any clear knowledge why it does so ; if it has several times seen young ones hatching from its eggs it is possible that a memory remains of this fact, so that then it will sit on the eggs with some vague idea of the young ones that will appear, without, of course, understanding anything about the physiological effect of its brooding. The effect of a former action, then, is no longer merely implicitly preserved in the strengthening or weakening of an innate instinctive activity, but experience may influence the animal's acts in a more explicit way, so that we may then have a greater right to speak of a striving, explicitly directed towards a goal. The originally purely instinctive action may thus reach the higher level of a willed action, of a *volition*.

The second point that we must stress is that, even if intelligence influences and rebuilds instincts and plays a part in the instinctive behaviour of an animal, it would nevertheless be erroneous to believe that its actions are now prompted by intelligence, an error often made especially in the case of man. It is always the instinct which provides the drive and the energy necessary to perform an action, intelligence only plays the secondary rôle of directing instinctively released actions in a special way. Intelligence-actions are a special case of instinctive actions ; behind the intelligence there is always the instinct which compels the animal to its actions.

And then, finally, the most important change which

intelligence imparts to an animal is that it places the individual on a higher level. An animal acting only under the drive of its instincts is no more than one of his species. By the working of its intelligence, by the after-effects of its own particular experience, a personal note comes to the fore. Intelligence transforms an animal to a personality among its congeners.

After these general considerations on the intelligence of animals we shall try to give a survey of the different forms of it found in the animal world. Although we begin with the simpler forms, we shall summarize them without pretending to give them in any hierarchical order or to construct a system in which each further type means a higher form of intelligence. Needless to say that here, as always where distinctions are made in matters of living nature, sharp distinctions cannot be made, and some cases might be classed equally well with one type as with another.

The *first form* we may distinguish, then, is that of *psychological habituation.* In the preceding chapter we saw that there is a habituation on a physiological basis, a simple physiological adaptation of the sense organs. There exists, besides this, a habituation based on acquired experience, although perhaps it will not always be possible to distinguish sharply between the two. The most marked, be it perhaps only a relative external difference between them, is that while physiological habituation is but temporary, psychological habituation may have a more permanent effect. The clearest example of such a habituation is provided by a wild animal living in a game reserve park, or captured by man and forced to live in his proximity. At first such an animal will show fear of men, and the sight of an approaching man will release its instinct of flight. When after some time it notices that no danger threatens from the side of man, and that its keeper even brings food and tends it, by this experience man will get a new valence for it and the sight of man will no more release the instinct of flight, but perhaps will even release the action of approaching the man in the expectation of getting food. Such a habituation may even occur in animals as low in the animal scale as larvæ of insects. Thus Sondheim brought larvæ of the dragon-fly Aeschna grandis so far as to accept flies from his hand, and even to come to the front of the aquarium as soon as he approached it.

Animals in this way may become habituated to all kinds of originally threatening perceptions. The Peckhams found in the case of females of the spider Epeira labyrinthica that they let themselves drop from their web if the experimenter approached with a vibrating tuning-fork. After some repetitions, however, this reaction disappeared. This habituation developed gradually ; an animal which the first time had let itself drop 15-18 inches and there waited for several minutes before venturing to climb up again into the web, after the seventh experiment evinced much less alarm and after some twenty experiments let itself drop only an inch or two and then came back at once. After the twenty-second experiment it merely lifted its forelegs if the vibrating fork was brought near to it. It is clear that this change cannot be regarded as a case of simple physiological adaptation of the sense organs ; here the animal must have learnt by experience that the vibration of the tuning fork did not imply impending danger from which it had to flee. Miss Fielde reports how her ants in an artificial nest gradually became tamer, did not allow themselves to be disturbed by the cleaning of the nest and after some time no longer stung her if they were touched. Brun succeeded in forming alliance-colonies between different species of ants (e.g., Formica rufa, pratensis and sanguinea) in which the animals almost completely ceased their original mutual hostilities. This was not due to the forming of a complex odour out of the odour of the component colonies, for the animals still distinguished their congeners from those of the other species, and members of their own nest were treated as friends, while those of the other part were attacked although only mildly. This habituation occurred especially in difficult or unusual situations, as, for instance, in the face of a common enemy.

An interesting case of such a psychological habituation was observed by tenCate-Kazejewa. The hermit-crab, Pagurus arrosor, lives in the shell of a snail. If the abdomen of the animal be touched through an opening in the shell it at first contracts within its shell, but after a stronger stimulation leaves the shell and crawls round till it finds shelter in another shell, sometimes its own. If, now this stimulation be repeated several times, the animal at the first slight touch on its abdomen immediately escapes out of the shell, but then remains in the neighbourhood of it and returns to it as soon as the stimulation has ceased. By experience the simple reaction of contraction on being touched is replaced by one of a real flight, but on the other hand the animal also has learnt by experience that the danger is soon over, and remains in the neighbourhood. By this it proves to be more or less habituated to the originally frightening sensation of being touched.

Habituation may, of course, also come about in the reverse direction. Animals in regions where no human beings occur first show no fear of them, as Darwin had already observed on his visit to the Galapagos Islands. Bitter experience, however, soon suffices to make them afraid of man. Although the term "habituation" does not seem to be very appropriate in this case the working of the intelligence in altering the animal's actions is in effect the same in both cases.

Habituation may be regarded as a negative effect of intelligence, that is, the animal learns to desist from a certain action. More positive effect is shown in a *second type of intelligence*, namely, that in which one perception comes by experience *to function as a signal* for another. We already found an example of this in the behaviour of Paramæcium, which learned by experience that light was a signal for an uncomfortable temperature of the water. Instances of this signal-forming are very numerous among the animals. The worm Nereis virens lives in a tube in the sand at the bottom of the sea. If, now, in the aquarium some meat be placed before the tube the feeding instinct of the worm is released, and it comes partially out of the tube in search of the food. If, on the other hand, light or shadow is cast upon the tube, the worm retires deeper into it by way of flight. Copeland, now, in a dark room threw a light on the animal, and 15—20 seconds later laid a piece of mussel before the tube. After a number of repetitions of this experiment the worm not only came out of the tube on the perception of the slowly-diffusing meat-juice, but reacted in a positive way as soon as it was stimulated by the light. By experience it had learnt to regard the light as a signal for the arrival of food coming, and the light released the feeding-instinct instead of the flight-instinct. A curious instance of such a signal-forming in lower animals was observed by Ada Yerkes. The tube-worm Hydroides dianthus contracts in its tube if a shadow is cast upon it. After some more shadowing this reaction ceases as the result of a physiological or psychological habituation. More regular and lasting is the reaction if no shadow is cast upon the animal but it is touched gently with a little rod. If Mrs. Yerkes let the shadowing be followed by a gentle touch, the reaction to the shadow did not stop, but the animal kept on contracting at the shadow. Here experience had taught that the shadow was a signal for the subsequent touching, so that the normal habituation was suspended.

As we stated above, examples of such signal-forming are numerous among the lower animals ; signal-forming is indeed the most common form of intelligence in them. But among the higher animals also signal-forming is a very common phenomenon. The carp in the fish-pond which approach the land when a man comes to the edge of the pond, having learnt by experience that the man brings food to them, the dog who has learnt that if his master is dressed in a particular way this is a signal for a walk for them both in the fields, and many other cases might be quoted as instances of such a signal-forming. The whole life of intelligent animals is full of such signals, perceptions standing for something else.

In this connection we must make a brief mention of the so-called *"conditioned reflexes."* That the term reflex, used by Pavlov and his followers, is in such cases mostly an inadequate indication of what really happens with the animal is a point we have already treated in a former chapter. It is certainly better to call these processes "conditioned responses," if it is preferred to keep to the term "conditioning" instead of using the more simple term of "learning." But apart from this question of terminology, we may say that these conditioned responses, too, are good examples of an intelligent signal-forming in animals, based on acquired experience. If one of Pavlov's dogs secretes saliva on hearing a bell ringing, it is because this ringing has been followed several times by the giving of food. The sound thus has become a signal for the forthcoming meal, and the secretion of saliva is part of the action of his feeding instinct, an anticipation of the following actions of seizing upon food and chewing it. The so-called conditioned reflexes of dogs and other animals involve intelligence on the part of these animals, and Pavlov's term "psychic salivation" expresses this feature of the phenomenon much better than that generally in use.

A *third type of intelligence* is found where experience creates a *distinction* between different perceptions which originally were not kept apart. We have already seen that the young mammal at first does not know where to suck, but sucks all that is warm and soft on his mother's body, her hair as well as her teats. But experience soon teaches him that sucking his mother's hair does not bring the desired appeasement, and that for this end the teats are the parts of her body to suck. This brings with it a distinction among the warm and soft parts ; some are likely to satisfy his hunger, others are not. Herewith the perception of the animal becomes more differentiated. A classical example of this learning to distinguish is presented by Morgan's experiments with chicks. Young chicks when newly hatched from the egg begin to pick at all small objects within their reach, whether they be grains of corn, or pebbles, or pieces of paper, or spots of light on the ground, or even their own toes. Experience soon teaches them, however, what can be picked up and what not, what is edible and what is not, what has a good and what has a bad taste. Intelligence thus brings more distinction into their perceptive world. Young animals, which at first do not generally know how to distinguish between innocent and dangerous creatures, learn this by experience with them or, as we saw, from the examples given by their parents. Especially the first hours of their life are for many animals often very important in this respect. Lorenz has shown that birds during the first hours of their life gather much experience especially with regard to their congeners, an experience which is preserved for their whole life and in his opinion can never be reversed. It may, however, well be doubted whether this view concerning the irreversibility of first experience is right and whether there is an essential difference between this early experience and that which is acquired later in life. Nevertheless, it is certain that birds during their first hours pass through a specially sensible period of their life, in which their intelligence is very active in the assimilation of lasting experience.

A further type of intelligence is that of the *formation of simple motor habits*. Jennings laid individuals of the starfish Asterias forreri on their back and then forced them to use a particular pair of arms in turning over again, by holding the other arms fast. One individual learnt in 180 experiments to use these arms only in three out of ten cases after all the arms were set free. Moore was able to train an Asterias to begin its reversal-movements with one particular arm by touching the other arms every time the animal tried to use them. A well-known example of such motor habits was given by Yerkes in his experiment with the earthworm Allolobophora foetida. He put this animal into a T-shaped tube of glass, the right arm of which ended in a dark wooden box, while the left arm was furnished with a piece of blotting paper soaked in a strong salt solution, or, in later experiments, with electrically charged copper wires. So by reward and punishment the animal had to learn to choose the right arm and to form the simple motor habit of turning to the right, every time it came to the point of bifurcation. This was attained rather quickly although the learning was not absolute and good days alternated with bad ones. These results of Yerkes were later corroborated by other experimenters, while similar motor habits, such as the choosing of the right or left way out of an apparatus, were formed also by other animals, like snails and crabs. From this simple choosing between a right and a left path there is a gradual transition to the learning by higher animals to follow intricate paths in a maze. The learning of these complicated paths, however, shows some aspects that are lacking in the learning of these

simple paths. We shall come back to this maze problem in
our next chapter.

As an example of the forming of such a simple motor
habit in a higher animal we may mention that of a guinea-pig,
trained by Grindley to turn his head to the right as soon as
a buzzer was switched on, which the animal learned by being
rewarded with a piece of carrot as soon as it did so.

These motor habits bring us to another type of the
modification of instinctive action by intelligence, viz., that
of the *acquirement of the necessary skill* in the performance
of such an action. In the preceding chapter we saw that the
improvement in instinctive action by practice may be based
on physiological as well as on psychological phenomena, and
that it is not always easy to say if only a physiological maturation is responsible for it, or if the improvement is the result
of experience concerning the effect of certain movements. In
that chapter we mentioned as such a doubtful case the
learning to fly by young cormorants. Young chickens that
from the earliest moments of life peck at small objects, do
not at first always get them. Their pecking, however, is soon
improved, and here again it is not easy to decide from the
partly contradictory results of different students how much
of this improvement must be ascribed to a physiological
maturation only and how much to the good or bad experience
gained during the pecking movements. That a bird of prey
profits by experience in the catching of his prey, that the
same is the case with the squirrel improving his leaping from
one branch of a tree to another, seems to leave no doubt.
One of the clearest examples of this improvement in an
instinctive action by experience is given by Lorenz with the
red-backed shrike (Lanius collurio). It is part of the instinctive equipment of this bird to impale insects and other small
animals on the thorns of branches. This behaviour is, however, not wholly innate ; innate is the drive to do so, but the
bird has to learn that this impaling must be done on thorns.
Young shrikes at first make the required movements with the
food in their bill, but at random anywhere in their cage, and
without paying attention to suitable places, such as nails or
thorns. But if the bird by accident has experienced that food

remains hanging on nails, these subjects will then be used in the performance of its innate instinctive activity.

A more complex phenomenon is that of *"homing"* in animals. Under a "home" we may understand all places which for some reason the animal desires to reach again after having left it, be it because it finds a shelter there, or food, or because its progeny has been left behind. The finding of its home, if this is not directly perceptible by vision or scent or some other sense perception, requires the help of former experience, in other words of intelligence. The lowest animal of which it is known that it possesses such a home and is able to find it again after leaving it is the limpet (Patella), a snail which lives on the rocks in the tidal zone of the coast and in rest occupies there a slight hollow in the stone corresponding exactly to the outline of its own shell. For long it has been known that each Patella has its own place on the rocks, towards which it returns after having left it to feed on the algæ of the rock. The problem now is, how the animal is able to find its own place again. This has proved to be rather a complex case. Patella does not simply retrace the tracks of its outward path. The direction of the light seems to play a certain, although not a preponderating part in the finding of the home again, in so far as the animal in returning may try to keep the light on the side other than that on which it was when it left its place. It seems that in the homing of Patella several kinds of experience are utilized : a general remembrance of the direction of the home with regard to the direction of the light ; a remembrance of the distance covered since the home was left ; but, above all, a general knowledge of the structure of the surroundings nearest its home, based on tactile perceptions of the surface of the rock. Out of all this a *"place-memory"* is formed, based on the experience obtained on former occasions about the meaning of special characteristics of the surroundings in finding its place again. This knowledge of the surroundings is of course limited ; it therefore need cause no wonder that if a Patella be taken away from her place and put down on the rocks at some distance from it, the greater this distance is, the fewer will be the number of snails which succeed in finding their way back.

This acquiring of a place-memory by perceiving and retaining impressions regarding the characteristics of the home surroundings is very marked in insects which possess such a home, be it bees, ants or wasps, living in communal nests, or fossorial wasps, for which the home is the place where they dug their nest for storing provisions for their future offspring. Before leaving such a place such animals are seen first to make orientation-flights around the nest, during which they get acquainted with the surroundings and learn to know plants and stones and other objects as landmarks to guide them on their way back. Displacement of such landmarks by the interference of man causes the animals to become confused and they are no longer able to find the nest again. It is not possible to review here the extensive literature on this homing in animals, but it will be clear that this homing must be regarded as another and somewhat more complicated type of animal intelligence.

As a last type of the lower forms of animal intelligence to be treated in this chapter, we must mention the so-called *"learning by trial and error,"* a term introduced by Morgan and generally adapted by students of animal psychology, although it would certainly have been better to name it a "learning by success and failure," as these two words express much better what really is the foundation of the learning which results from it.

This learning by trial and error, then, takes place in the following way. An animal finds itself confronted with a special task which it wishes to accomplish, e.g., to reach some place, mostly because food is to be found there, or to free itself from some confinement, or to do some other thing which an instinct impels it to do. This it tries to attain by making some movements or performing some actions which, although they are directed towards this end, are mostly at first merely accidental. It may then happen that most of these movements or actions are unsuccessful and do not further its aim, but one, or some, of them bring it to the end desired. The unsuccessful movements then get clothed with the negative feeling of being ineffectual ; those which were successful with the positive feeling of bringing the animal nearer to its goal. In the way described above the latter movements are stamped in, and the former will be omitted, if another time the animal finds itself in the same situation.

A classical example of this learning by trial and error is provided by Thorndike's experiments with cats and dogs in his problem-boxes. In these experiments the animals were confronted with a problem which originally lay beyond their capacities to solve. They had to open a box or case closed by a complicated mechanism, in which a handle had to be turned, or a latch had to be lifted, or a loop had to be pulled down; or sometimes a combination of these manipulations had to be performed, in order to free themselves from a cage in which they were confined, or to open a box in order to reach food. At first therefore their movements were quite haphazard, but by selecting the successful ones out of all those that were made the animals as a rule sooner or later got so far as to be able to open the box at once by making the required movements. From the results obtained Thorndike drew some conclusions regarding the intelligence of his animals which were not very flattering to them, but were partly unjust and certainly were over-generalized. They were subsequently much criticized, and it is therefore needless to dwell upon them here.

Much of the behaviour of higher animals, seemingly based on understanding, is undoubtedly no more than the result of such learning by trial and error. A good example of this was provided by one of Morgan's dogs. This animal, if let free in the garden, was wont to stand on a parapet wall and look through the railing to see what happened in the street. Once when, accidentally, he looked out under the latch of the gate, he happened to raise his head, so that the latch was lifted and the gate swung open. At first the dog did not notice what he had done, but as he saw the gate opened he went out of the garden into the street. According to Morgan's description, after some ten or twelve of these casual occurrences, in which the dog's exit from the garden was gradually effected with greater speed and with less gazing out at wrong places, he learnt by experience to go straight to the right place and there make directly the right movement. To a passer-by, then, it might have seemed as if the dog had at once performed the right action with a clear understanding of the effects of his raising the latch, but to one who, like Morgan, had followed the whole process of learning, it is clear that this performance developed gradually by a strengthening of accidentally successful movements.

This learning by trial and error leads us to a higher type of animal intelligence than any hitherto described. If a dog, like that of Morgan's, learns only by experience to execute one particular movement at one particular place to attain one particular end, this process cannot be estimated much higher than the learning of a crab to move to the right side at a bifurcation of the path, or even that of a worm coming out of its tube in order to get food if a shadow is cast on it. But are performances like these the best an animal can show ? Might not the animal be able in some cases to understand more explicitly the results of its own actions during those trials, and to apply them to other cases more or less dissimilar from those in which this experience was originally gathered ? If this were the case, we should have to admit that there might be more in such a performance than the plain execution of an action that has been stamped in by experience of its results ; some real understanding might in fact be involved in its actions. It will be our task in the next chapter to discuss whether anything like such understanding is actually exhibited in animal behaviour, whether an animal ever carries out with understanding a purposive action which is not innate, whether in other words we can find in the animals something more akin to what at the beginning of this chapter we described as intelligence in man.

CHAPTER V

THE PROBLEM OF ANIMAL UNDERSTANDING

W E ended the preceding chapter by describing how, by a process known as "trial and error," an animal may come to the proper performance of some particular, not innate, actions, necessary to reach an end towards which it is driven by an instinct, as for instance the opening of a box in order to get food or the unlocking of a garden-gate in order to get out. We then asked if this was the highest pitch that animal intelligence could reach. We may now answer this question by saying that it is not, but that, be it by this "trying and erring" or in another way, some of the more gifted among the animals may attain to a form of intelligence that we must consider as a higher type than that of only giving new or other valences to their actions ; to put it more accurately, we can state that some animals can in fact arrive at a real understanding of the means necessary to reach a desired end.

Of what does this understanding consist, and how is it attained ? The answer must be that this understanding is based on *the noticing of the essential elements in a situation, and the grasping of their mutual relations with regard to the end desired*, followed by the ability to apply this knowledge in order to reach the goal. But here again we must realize that it is not necessary to assume that in such cases the animal forms explicit ideas of these elements and their relations, that it explicitly forms connections between them in its mind, that it judges and thinks. Here again the whole process takes place on a lower, more immediate, level ; it is rather a direct sensorial insight than the result of prior deliberation, more a *"seeing"* than a *"thinking."* Further, the understanding takes place on the level of the concrete, i.e. of the spatial and the temporal, and the abstract is not involved. For this reason we will term this form of animal intelligence *"concrete understanding."*

It will be clear that, in order to obtain such an understanding, an animal requires a certain endowment, be it a specific or an individual one. Some species are better endowed, are cleverer, than others, but also within one species different degrees of endowment may be found. Even animals of the same litter may differ in this regard. Age and psychical maturation also play a rôle in this endowment : older animals, with much experience, are often cleverer than younger ones. The cunning of an old fox is proverbial. But even without particular experience the ability to grasp such relations may increase with age. Lorenz reports that young jackdaws which had at first been unable immediately to make a detour through a door, although they several times found their way through it by trial and error, after being caged up for four weeks at once took the right way. As practice in this case was precluded, the increase of understanding can only be ascribed to psychical growth.

As in other similar cases, it is not possible to draw a line anywhere in the animal realm and assert that below this line only the lower forms of intelligence are found, whereas above the line a real understanding may also manifest itself. Higher and lower grades of intelligence cannot be sharply distinguished, higher and lower forms of intelligence may work together in the performance of intelligent actions by the same animal. If we let animals run through a simple or a more complicated maze, where does the frontier lie between the simple learning of a motor habit, as was the case with Yerkes' earthworm, and the real understanding of the path it has to follow, as we shall presently describe it in higher animals like rats ? Insects, in particular, with their instincts, on the one hand so complicated and on the other so often subject to regulation, frequently show behaviour which a casual observer would perhaps be inclined to ascribe to understanding, but which we shall probably do better not to value so highly. The Peckhams once observed a Pompilus enlarging the opening of her nest as it appeared that the spider she was bringing with her was too big to be got into it. Must we ascribe this to insight on the part of the wasp that the dislodging of some sand would remove the hindrance to bringing the spider into the nest ? Or must we believe that to enlarge the opening belongs to the instinctive equipment of the species, so that every Pompilus instinctively adapts the dimensions of the nest-opening to that of her prey ? It is difficult to decide this. Some authors, like Hingston, have been rather generous in ascribing all such behaviour to insight. It would seem better to remain somewhat more critical and, for the rest, leave the answering of this question open till more knowledge respecting the instinctive endowment of the species is available.

Now, the basis of all such understanding is the experience gathered by the animal in the course of its life, as we have described this in our preceding chapter. From its first day onwards the animal has to deal with all kinds of objects and situations. In this way it acquires experience about their properties, about the distances and directions of particular places, about the hardness and impenetrability of certain objects, about the results of its own intervention in situations. The young chicken learns by experience that if it turns round that wall it will reach the garden ; the young monkey that if he draws a branch towards him, the leaves and fruit on that branch will follow the movement. According to its intellectual endowment, it learns by this more or less to understand the relation between different events. Then the circumstances, or the caprice of the experimenter, place the animal in a situation not encountered before. None of the higher animals of a certain age comes quite unprepared into such a situation ; each brings with it some experience which may now be a help to it. If, as we supposed, this new situation is not quite identical with those which the animal has met with before, there will yet be some similarity between the new situation and the former ones. What will happen now depends on the ability of the animal to see the agreement between the essential elements of both situations and to apply its former experience of those elements to the new situation. The outcome of this, then, may be different. First it may be that the animal directly sees through the new situation, and with the help of its former experience immediately finds the right solution of the problem which confronts it. The chicken sees the new opening in the wall and goes through it into the garden ; the monkey draws in the rope on which the experi-menter has fixed a piece of food. We then say that the animal has shown a *"primary solution"* of the problem, although in the strict sense of the word the term "primary" is not quite adequate, as the solution in such cases is the result of experi-ence gathered in former more or less similar situations. If there is no such primary solution, two things may happen. First the animal may wholly fail to find the solution and after some futile attempts give up the problem before which it is placed. But it is also possible that the animal begins to try different means and so by purposive trials sooner or later comes to the desired solution, as we have already described in our former chapter. This, then, may be called a "*secondary solution.*" It will be clear that the difference between a primary and a secondary solution is only relative, and not so essential as has been believed by authors who, like Köhler, reserve the term "insight" to those primary solutions, especially if these appear suddenly and unexpectedly. There may be several reasons for such a sudden solution, reasons that have nothing to do with intelligence as such. The animal, for instance, may suddenly and accidentally perceive something it did not perceive before, or the animal may suddenly for some reason be brought to hasten its action. But even if the understanding does suddenly arise, there is no reason to attach to this understanding an essentially different character. Primary and secondary solutions show only quantitative differences ; the now primary solution owes its primarity to previous secondary ones. There may be a primary and a secondary insight, but both are insight.[1] Primary and secondary solutions are, indeed, not always clearly distinguishable ; before an animal shows a so-called primary solution it may have performed small actions that smooth the path for the final solution, and the decision, whether something is done primarily or secondarily may sometimes be difficult. But the result is the same : whether by a primary or by a secondary solution, the animal executes the actions necessary to reach its end. And the shorter its trials on the next occasion when it is placed in a similar situation, the better was its understanding in the first case.

The question may now be asked, what kind of mutually related elements of a situation may be grasped in this way by the animals, and what forms of concrete understanding do we therefore meet in them. The answer must be that these elements are of a threefold nature. First, the animal may grasp the *relation between spatial elements* in its world,

---

[1] Some authors speak of "*insight-learning*" if this embraces more than a mechanical stamping in of some movements. This, however, is wrong : insight may be the result of learning, but it is not a mode of learning itself.

the relation of a "next-to-each-other" or "before-and-behind-each-other" of elements. Then, the animal may grasp the *relation between temporal elements*, the relation of a "before-and-after-each-other" of elements. And, thirdly, it may grasp *causal relations*, the relation of "cause-and-effect" between phenomena. We will now demonstrate these three types of concrete understanding by some examples.

Let us begin with the *spatial relations*. Here we may distinguish between two different types of situation, according as such relations are either existing independently of, or arise only during, the movements of an animal and in relation to these. For convenience sake we may distinguish them as *"static"* and *"kinetic"* relations of space.

As an example of the first we may quote the experiments made by Yerkes in his so-called "multiple-choice-apparatus." This apparatus consists of a number of similar boxes, placed next to each other in a row or a sector of a circle. First Yerkes used twelve such boxes, later nine, but this number, of course, is immaterial. In each experiment a number of the boxes were closed and thus put out of use, while the remaining ones were left open. The number of the open boxes changed with each experiment, and so did their place in the whole apparatus ; thus one time a number of them at the right side of the row were left open, another time a different number at the left side, a third time again another in the middle, and so on. The task for the animal, now, was to choose one box among those left open, which was characterized by its relative position among the open boxes, as for instance the first one on the left, or the second on the right, or the middle one in an uneven number, etc. As the number and the place of the open boxes were changed after each experiment it was not possible for the animal to direct itself towards some more simple absolute characteristics, as for instance for distance of the box from the edge of the apparatus, or the place of the box in the room, or such like.

In order to make a comparative test between a number of different animals with this apparatus, Yerkes had devised ten different tasks with an increasing degree of difficulty.

The easiest task was, of course, to choose the first box on the right or the left. A more difficult task was to choose the second box in the row, or the middle one. Still more difficult for the animal was to choose alternatively the first box on the right and the second on the left, as herein also another factor, viz. that of time, was involved. It soon became evident that all these more complicated tasks were too difficult for the animals ; only with the most simple ones were good results obtained. Curiously enough, relatively the best results were obtained, not with monkeys or even anthropoids, but with birds. A Macacus cynomolgus of Yerkes learned to choose the first on the left in 150 experiments, and to choose the second on the right in 1,080 experiments, but as he still made errors when new combinations of boxes were opened, it appeared that he had learned rather to choose the correct box in a special number of combinations than to choose according to the principle required. A Rhesus monkey learned somewhat more quickly, and, in 480 experiments learned to choose alternatively the first on the left and the second on the right. Trying to teach him to choose the middle box in a varying uneven number of boxes met with no success in 320 experiments. With anthropoids the results were no better. An Orang did not get farther than choosing the first on the left, while of four chimpanzees only one was able to learn to choose alternatively the outermost boxes, and none to choose the middle box.

Somewhat better were the results with lower animals and birds. Two swine of Yerkes and Coburn learnt to choose the first box on the right and the second on the left, and even alternatively the first on the right and the first on the left, but to choose the middle box was again too difficult. Two crows learned no more than to choose the first on the right ; but better results were obtained by Sadovinkova with song-birds, which rather quickly learnt the easier problems, and of which a siskin even learnt to choose the middle box in different combinations. Later the author tried whether better results would be obtained with monkeys if the boxes were arranged, not in a horizontal but in a vertical row, but his results were not much better than those of Yerkes.

It appears thus that learning such static relations of space is rather difficult for the animal. This is not surprising. In nature an animal is never placed before such a task, so that the endowment and probably even the attention to the solution of such problems is lacking in them. Better results, however, are obtained if spatial relations are to be grasped while the animal is in movement, a task more in harmony with its natural needs.

Grasping the relation between spatial elements while in movements is necessary when an animal is forced to make a *detour*, a round-about way, if the direct road to its goal is blocked, or has occasion to take a short cut, if the possibility arises to shorten the usual way by the absence of some customary obstacle. It will be clear that these are problems with which an animal is often confronted in its natural life, where the direct way to the nest, or to some prey perceived, is not always possible, and the animal must try to reach it by a longer indirect way.

It may be thought that, perhaps, to make such a detour offers scarcely any difficulty to an animal, and that any animal which is able to obtain a total impression of a certain area is also able to make the necessary detours in this area. That such is not the case was shown by the author's experiments with Octopus. When the animals were lying in a corner of the aquarium he put a short distance away a small wire-netting, and behind this a live crab, the favourite food of the octopus. Although it appeared that the animals clearly distinguished the edges of the network and so quite easily could have reached the crab by creeping round it or stretching out one of their long arms, none of them did so, but all tried in vain to take the direct way to the prey through the wire netting. Nor were they able to catch a live crab out of a tumbler set in the aquarium, but continued to bump against the glass instead of putting an arm into it. It must be mentioned that Buytendyk, when repeating these experiments with a number of octopus, found that one of them, after many failures to reach the crab in the direct way, suddenly crept round the wire netting and seized the crab. This shows how the endowment for the solution of this problem may vary in animals of the same species ; probably in this case the task lies at the limit of their ability.

But higher animals as a rule are able to make detours, be it directly, in a primary solution of the problem, or secondarily, after a longer or shorter process of trying. When surveying the literature on this problem we see that there are *four different types of detours* with increasing degree of difficulty. To the *first type* belong such detours in which both the goal and the way to it can be seen from the starting point, and in which there is then no need for the animal to turn its back to the goal during its march towards it and so lose it from sight for some moments. The *second type* is that in which at the starting-point the goal is visible and the road to it can be seen, but in which during part of the march the animal is forced to turn its back to the goal. The *third type* is such that the goal is visible from the starting-point, but the path cannot be seen and must be guessed more or less from former experience. And a *fourth degree of difficulty* is given, if the path not only cannot be seen from the starting-point, but even the goal is not visible from there, so that the animal must know from former experience that the goal (food or such like) is to be found within the apparatus. We will show by some examples how animals deal with the four types of detours.

A detour of the first type we have found already in the path the octopus has to take in order to reach the crab that it saw before it, and which could be kept in view while going to it. Other examples can easily be imagined : the dog that sees his master standing outside the garden runs first to the open gate and from there to his master. To quote another example with invertebrates : Drzewina made use of the positive phototaxis of a crab to make the animals move from the darker part of an aquarium into a part illuminated by a lighted candle, in doing which they had to pass through an opening at one side of the glass partition which divided the aquarium into two. The first day four animals found the right way in 1, 5, 15 and 35 minutes respectively after several bumps against the glass-plate. By the third day, however, they went directly through the opening, in from ten seconds to two minutes. In this case the burning candle or the illuminated part of the aquarium could be kept constantly in view. With various fishes similar detour experiments have been made with like results.

That the making of a detour is made difficult to some animals if the goal is lost sight of for a time was clearly demonstrated by Fischel in experiments with lizards. If, when in making their detour, these animals had to pass round a piece of cardboard, so that the food they were trying to reach was invisible for some moments, most of them stopped there, or forgot the food, and only went to it if later they saw the food again by accident. How variously different animals may behave in such circumstances was shown by Köhler in his experiments with dogs and chickens. These animals were brought into a cul-de-sac 2 m. long and 1 m. broad, and closed with wire netting, behind which food was laid. A dog showed a primary solution of this problem, turned round, and went without stopping out of the cul and round a fenced-in piece of ground straight to the food. Chickens, on the other hand, were not able to do this, even if a shorter detour was required than in the case of the dog, but kept running to and fro before the network. Only gradually did some of them succeed in finding the way to the food. If Köhler had carried on his experiments with his chicks there would certainly have come a moment in which these too would have been able to make the proper detour, after a longer or shorter period of trying. This shows that a problem, which can be solved primarily by one animal, with another requires a longer or shorter time of trying, and is solved only secondarily.

That even higher animals may find it difficult to make a detour if having first to move away from the goal, was shown by the author with monkeys and lemurs. These animals had to make two detours. The first one was, when sitting on the top of a large bird-cage, to climb down and enter the cage in order to reach the food the experimenter was offering them there. The other one was, when sitting on a branch in that cage, to get down from it to the floor of the cage and to go out of it and to climb up outside it in order to reach the food the experimenter was offering them above the cage. Monkeys found no difficulty in solving these two problems. Lemurs, on the other hand, had no difficulty with the first problem but did with the second. They always tried to snatch the food through the bars of the cage and only reached it if, after having given up trying and having left the cage, they happened to see the food from outside the cage and then went to it. After repeating this experiment several times they finally learned to make the right detour directly, which, in this case, was learned as a secondary fusion of two originally separate actions. The cause of this unequal difficulty in the two problems was obvious : in the second problem the animals had to turn their backs to the food while descending from their perch.

Other animals, however, showed better performances when they had to make even more difficult detours. The cats of Adams, the rats of Maier, the dogs of Hobhouse made complicated detours to a point, where they saw food lying or their master standing, along paths which were not visible from the starting point and while during their walk to the goal they had repeatedly to lose sight of this goal. Sarris got good results with dogs when he ordered them to go to a point known to them but not visible from the starting place, as for instance their basket, even if they had to cover a complicated path in order to reach it. That tree-animals, like monkeys and beech martens, find no difficulty in making perpendicular detours, too difficult for ground-animals like dogs and polecats, might be expected and has been confirmed by experiments of Müller and others.

In close affinity to the making of detours is that of taking *short cuts*. Here, too, the relation of spatial elements must be grasped. Animals which have a nest, or a hole, generally know the spatial relations in the neighbourhood of this place and know how to return to it by the shortest way from every point in the surroundings, without being obliged to follow the frequently complicated path they took when leaving the nest. This is even the case with animals like ants and wasps. Hunting animals, like dogs and wolves, are often seen to cut off the path to the prey and so catch it at a point not yet reached by the prey at the moment when the short cut was made. In experiments in which rats were trained to follow a complicated path in an apparatus, they often showed themselves able to take a short cut if, after having learned the way, occasion was given to them to do so.

We mentioned just now experiments made by Sarris with dogs that had to find their way to a point which they could not see from the starting-point, but which they knew from former occasions. This fourth degree of difficulty in making detours is now being specially studied in a type of apparatus called a *maze*.

These mazes are too well known to require detailed description ; and the results of maze experiments are too numerous to make it possible to give a full account of them here. We may briefly define a maze as an apparatus consisting of a complicated system of alleys, some coming to a dead end and some leading to a goal in the centre of the apparatus, where some reward, mostly in the form of food, is to be found. The T-tube used by Yerkes with the earthworm may be regarded as the simplest type of such a maze. To follow the right path in a maze it is thus necessary to make a complicated detour, a detour so complicated that it is impossible for the animal to arrive at a primary solution—the more so as it has first to learn that there is in the apparatus a goal worth reaching (because food is to be found there), while, further, the path to this goal can never be seen in its entirety. White rats in particular have given evidence of being able to learn very intricate types of mazes. What is of more interest to us here is that the animal in learning the path through the maze has often proved that this involves more than a mere blind and mechanical following of a particular route. Often rats have shown themselves to possess some image of the road to be followed, and of the relations of a certain point in the maze to the position of the goal. For instance, they often seemed to have a feeling for the direction of the goal and a desire to move in that direction : they thus made more errors by entering blind alleys pointing in the direction of the goal than by entering those pointing in the opposite direction. If at some place they had to turn to the right or the left, they frequently made errors by anticipating these turnings and thus entering a preceding alley. Occasionally they also showed some understanding of the distance they were from the goal at some point of the maze. As we mentioned above, they sometimes manifested the capacity to take short cuts if they got the occasion to do so. At times they also appeared to have grasped the relation between parts of the apparatus, as was the case in an experiment of Hsiao, in which rats understood that if one door to the goal was closed, all alleys leading to this door had consequently to be avoided, and that they would have to make a detour to another door that would lead to the goal. All this demonstrates once again the capacity of certain animals to grasp spatial relations, even in such unfavourable conditions as are involved when they are forced to run through a maze.

Experiments on the capacity of animals to grasp *temporal relations* have revealed a much poorer ability than in the case of spatial relations. This need not excite wonder. Time plays a much less important part in animal life, and for this reason their attention is directed much less towards time and temporal elements. Here again we may distinguish between a *"static"* and a *"kinetic"* way of grasping such relations. Like Yerkes, who, with his multiple-choice-apparatus, studied the capacity of the animals to choose a box which was distinguished by its relative place in a row, Atkins and Dashiell investigated the question whether rats were able to learn to choose a door which was distinguished by its place in a temporal sequence. This was done in the following way. Three out of four doors in an apparatus were illuminated every time for a moment in varying order ; in one experiment the doors Nos. 4, 2, and 3 ; in the next the doors Nos. 2, 3, and 1, and so on. Then three out of twelve rats had to learn to enter the door that was illuminated first, six others to enter the door illuminated second, and three again to enter the door illuminated last. The result of these experiments was quite negative. In about 400 experiments no rat had learned this task, but they all formed position habits, i.e. they always chose the same door, or chose the doors in a fixed order. The results, therefore, showed an ability inferior to those revealed in Yerkes' experiments.

Somewhat better were the results if animals had *to do something in relation to a sequence of time*. That is to say, if they had to do first one thing, then another thing, and then again some other thing. The simplest example of this is *alternation*, when an animal has to do something, then another thing, then the first thing again, and so on. Thus Carr placed rats in an apparatus which they had to leave alternately through a door on the right and one on the left side, in order to reach a place where food was to be found. His eight animals learned this with great difficulty ; it was only after 400 experiments that the choice made was right in 85% cases. When, afterwards, Carr lengthened the intervals between two experiments from 16 seconds to one minute, the results became much poorer still. Another type of alternation was studied by Hunter. In an apparatus of T-form rats had to learn to choose alternately the right and the left exit in order to reach food. This was learned rather quickly, but when the animals had to learn the double alternation (*l-l-r-r-l-l-r-r-l-l*) in 500-600 experiments none of the rats could master this. Even the simple combination l-l-r-r could not be mastered by any of them in 200 experiments. Such a double alternation was apparently too difficult for them.

This was also shown by Hunter in his so-called "temporal maze." This apparatus consists of a central alley, at the end of which the animals can turn either to the right or to the left and so again come back through a side-alley to the starting point, from where they can again follow the central alley, and so on. Hunter, in this maze, tried to teach rats to run the double alternation *l-l-r-r-l-l-r-r-l-l*. This again was too difficult for them. Of as many as seven other rats which had to learn the simple alternation *l-r-l-r-l-r-l-r*, only one succeeded to a certain degree in 59 experiments.

It must be admitted, however, that other animals proved to be able to do more in such alternation experiments. Four raccoons of Hunter could not learn a fourfold double alternation (*r-r-l-l-r-r-l-l*), but were able more or less to learn the two-fold double alternation *r-r-l-l.* Two young Rhesus-monkeys of Gellerman learned the double alternation *r-r-l-l* in 80 and 315 experiments respectively, and similar results were obtained by Karn with cats. And when Karn and Patton taught this double alternation to cats, and then brought them to a similar temporal maze of different dimensions, the cats were able to perform their task in this new maze as well, which shows that their performance was based on an understanding of temporal relations, and not on some simple physiological phenomenon, as perhaps might be supposed.

In another way the author trained animals to perform similar rhythmic actions. When an inverted tin was placed on a table beside his cage, a monkey was trained to overturn this the first two times the tin was placed there, and to omit this the third time. (The first two times food was put under the tin and the third time not.) The animal thus was trained on a *"yes-yes-no"*-rhythm. This was learned in about 650 experiments, but when the interval between the experiments was lengthened from 10 to 20 seconds, the animal made 3 errors in 10 experiments, and when the interval was extended to 30 seconds it made 9 errors in 10 experiments. Doubling the interval, therefore, partly destroyed the acquired rhythm of action ; trebling it destroyed the rhythm almost entirely. If, on the other hand, an animal was trained on the more simple rhythm *"yes-no,"* a doubling of the interval had no influence, while with an interval of 30 seconds 6 errors were made in a series of 10 experiments, and with an interval of 45 seconds, 10 errors. A simpler rhythm apparently can admit of a greater change in the interval than a more complicated one. Another monkey could even be trained to a yet more complicated rhythm, viz., that of *"yes-yes-yes-no."*

Such rhythms of action were also learned in other ways. Rats of Ellis in a choice-apparatus learned to jump down three times to the right side and then once to the left. Koehler and his collaborators trained pigeons to pick up only a certain number out of a greater number of grains and to leave the others alone. First the animals learned to pick up 2 grains out of rows of from 3 to 6 ; finally, one bird came so far as to be able to pick up 6 grains out of a row of 7 to 13 and let the others alone. Although not all Koehler's results can perhaps be explained by admitting such rhythms of action, yet most of them do. Anyhow, it is certain that they cannot be ascribed to any *counting* on the part of the animals, as has been supposed by some authors. For real counting it would be necessary to possess the concepts of number, and no animal is able to form such concepts. Yet all the results mentioned in this section point to a more or less successful grasping of temporal relations. For, if an animal knows the right path to follow in a temporal maze, or turns a tin in a required sequence, or picks up some grains and leaves the others alone, it must have understood the "after-each-other" of certain actions it has to perform, i.e., it must have understood that the action *a* must be followed by the action *b*, and that after the action *p* all action must stop. This understanding of temporal relations may not go very far in animals, yet it is certain that in some of them it exists to a certain degree.

More interesting, however, are the results obtained with animals regarding their understanding of *causal relations*.

The first systematic experiments on this grasping of causal relations by animals were made by Thorndike with his problem-boxes, already mentioned in the preceding chapter. His dogs and cats had to open boxes with an intricate opening mechanism, too complicated to be understood by the animals at first sight. That the results were rather poor, and that the conclusions drawn by Thorndike from his results as to the understanding of the animals were not very favourable for the latter was, therefore, rather the fault of Thorndike than of his animals, the more so indeed inasmuch as Thorndike was somewhat prejudiced against them and even tried to explain away physiologically facts which actually did speak for some understanding on the part of his animals. Even in monkeys Thorndike could find no trace of real understanding. Later, however, other experimenters, working with other animals, obtained better results than Thorndike, even with similar problem-boxes. Raccoons of the McDougalls very soon learned to open a box closed with a vertical latch, either by pushing the latch away with a paw or with their nose. Then a second latch was fixed which held the first one, so that to open the box first the second latch and then the first latch had to be pushed aside. After this was learned a third and a fourth latch were fitted, and so on, till finally the box was closed by a system of 24 horizontal and vertical interlocking latches, distributed over the different walls of the box. One of the raccoons learned very quickly every time to open the new latch, and to push away all the latches in the proper order. With every new latch that was fitted, he understood almost at once the additional hindrance it formed to the opening of the other latches. He was also able to discover what was wrong if the latch was not sufficiently moved. His dexterity in opening the latches gradually improved, showing that during the work his understanding was increased by new experience. In a similar way rats of the McDougalls learned to open boxes with 14 latches, also to be undone in a certain order.

To study the understanding by animals of causal relations there are, however, better methods than the use of problem-boxes with their intricate closing-mechanisms, namely, the study of their handling of different objects, as this was first started by Hobhouse. We may divide these experiments into three groups : those of the *clearing away of obstacles*, those of the *utilising the possibilities of moving objects*, and those of the *use of tools*. Of each of these groups we will now give some examples.

With regard to the clearing away of obstacles, we may distinguish between obstacles which hamper the animals themselves in their movements, and those which stand in their way when trying to reach some goal. In both cases it is necessary that the animal should first recognize the obstacle as such, and then understand what to do in order to overcome it. On the first type some early experiments were carried out by Hobhouse. When the chain of a Rhesus monkey was laid round a box so that the monkey could not reach food laid on the floor, the animal immediately pushed the box away and so showed he understood that it was the box which hampered his movements, and that he had to push it away in order to be able to reach the food. Another time Hobhouse laid the chain round a heavy table. Then, after an interval, the animal managed to help himself by going around the other side of the table, in other words, by making a detour. In similar circumstances a pig-tailed macaque (Nemestrinus nemestrinus) of McDougall knew how to help himself in the same way, and if his chain was looped round a stake, he tried, sometimes with success, to lift the chain over the stake. A raccoon of McDougall in such a case even drew the stake out of the ground and then ran for the food. A good solution was presented by a rat of Schaff and Sgonina, which, when a rope held him from his goal, took the rope between his paws and gnawed it through. All these results show an understanding of how to deal with obstacles.

The same was often the case with objects which stood in the way of the animals when trying to reach a goal. Here again the first experiments were made by Hobhouse. A stool was placed before the door of a dog's kennel. After a slight hesitation the dog clawed the stool away and entered the kennel. Köhler repeated the same experiment with chimpanzees and put a box inside the cage of the animals just in front of the place where they had to reach for a banana laid outside the cage. His results, curiously enough, were rather disappointing. Not one of his six animals directly manifested the proper insight, and it was only after some futile endeavours to reach the fruit in another way that they gradually found the right solution. This is the more remarkable, inasmuch as the present author, in comparative experiments confronting different animals with a similar situation, obtained much better results from many of them. A pig-tailed macaque, a Cebus monkey, a young coati and a raccoon, all directly took the box and pushed or threw it away ; other monkeys and Lemurs did the same sooner or later after some had first tried to reach to food in another way, and only a squirrel did not get further than making a direct attack on the bars of the cage. This proves that it would be wrong to believe that the intelligence of animals correlates highly with their place in the animal system, and it warns us especially against the belief that in all such experiments chimpanzees must

9

give the best results, just because morphologically they most resemble man and are therefore placed at the top of the system. We may also mention here that a raven of Hertz drew a stone out of an opening if food was laid behind it. That many animals, even birds, are able to turn over a box or tin if they have seen food placed under it, may also be mentioned as a case of clearing away obstacles in order to reach a goal.

A great number of experiments with many animals have been performed to see whether they were able to use the possibility of some object being moved in order to reach a goal, in most cases, again, food. In this problem, too, experience in their daily life may help them. Every animal which has the power to set some object moving has the opportunity to observe that everything fixed on this object moves in the same direction. As we remarked already, a monkey which, in play, draws the branch of a tree towards him may notice that the leaves of the branch follow the movement, and the same is the case with the dog that pushes away his food-trough and may notice that the food it contains is pushed away with it. The question, whether an animal understands that in order to get at some object it must first move another object to which the former one is fixed, is therefore not an unreasonable one. Some authors have regarded such actions as examples of the using of tools. We believe it better to reserve this name for cases in which an animal itself actively brings an object into contact with the desired food and thereupon uses it for obtaining the food. Cases such as we will now describe might, then, be called examples of a *"spurious use of tools."* We find them to be of three types : that of *drawing in some object*, that of *pushing some object away* and that of *rotating some object*, all in order to reach the otherwise unattainable food.

In the first case, then, the animal has to draw an object towards it in order to obtain something attached to it. To study this problem food may be fastened to a cord, the one end of which lies within the reach of the animal, whereas the food itself lies beyond its reach. The cord with the food may also be hung on a branch on which the animal is sitting, so that it must pull up the cord in order to get the food. Instead of a cord a thin lath may be used, with food lying on one end. The task is somewhat more difficult for the animal if a little rake be used, which is laid behind the food, so that the animal must draw in the rake and so rake up the food. Apes, as well as monkeys and lemurs, generally find no difficulty in solving this problem and immediately draw in the cord or the lath. With other animals, however, the results of such experiments were rather different, and as a rule less good than with monkeys. It must be kept in mind, however, that the lower animals are less well equipped for such work than monkeys with their supple hands, and have to do it with their feet or teeth. Yet most of these animals, like the raccoons and coatis, or the rats and guinea-pigs of different experimenters, understood fairly well how to help themselves. The same was found in experiments with a fox, while with dogs and cats varying results were obtained. Some of these animals failed entirely, while others learned to do it after various trials, or even pulled in the cord at once.

This drawing in of a cord is rendered more difficult if the cord be laid round a pole so that, when the animal draws the cord in, the food first moves away, or if the cord be laid on the floor in loops, so that drawing in the cord at first does not make the food approach. Yet this did not discourage the cats of Adams and the monkeys of Guillaume and Meyerson from continuing to pull. Drawing in a cord with food has even been performed by birds (crows, parrots, different singing-birds) and may be observed in the garden when titmice sit on a tree and draw up a string with a peanut some bird-friend has hung there for their food.

The raking in of food, if the rake is laid behind it, is not generally a very difficult task for an animal able to draw in anything at all. Even squirrels can do so. This, however, lasts only as long as the food moves with the movement of the rake. If it happens that the food slips from the rake, or if the rake is laid, not behind, but beside the food, no animal, as a rule, with the exception of anthropoid apes, is able, on his own initiative, to get the rake behind the food again. At best we see only some vague movements with the rake in the direction of the food. In such cases more is required from the animal, viz. the capacity to use an object as a real tool. We shall return to this question presently.

Much more difficult is it for an animal to push something away, in order to get it after making a short detour. The difficulty here is, of course, that in pushing, the food moves away in a direction opposite to that wanted by the animal. To study this, food is laid inside a tube with a stick partly projecting from it, between the food and the animal, so that the animal must push the food through the tube in order to get it. Even for monkeys this problem is mostly too difficult ; only some chimpanzees learned to do it, and some of them were even able to push the food out of the tube with a stick laid beside it, which implied the understanding of the use of a tool.

A third type utilizing the possibilities of moving objects lies in rotation. The method employed to study whether animals understand how to make use of rotation is to fix a lath on a hinge, so that it can be rotated in a vertical or horizontal direction, and to lay food on its free end beyond the animal's reach. A rotating plate also may be used, on the farther end of which food is laid. The latter task is some-what more difficult than the former, as the animal must learn not to try to draw the plate to it, as is its natural tendency, but to make it turn and to continue the movement till the food is within its reach. Monkeys and lemurs generally solve this problem primarily, as soon as the possibility of rotating the plate is noticed by them. So do raccoons, and coatis, while with cats the results once again varied greatly, and a squirrel belonging to the author did not get farther than biting the plate. The problem can be rendered still more difficult if a lath has to be rotated around a vertical axis, fixed in the middle of the lath. Then the food moves away in a direction opposite to that of the end of the lath which the animal has set in motion. Even the chimpanzees of Guillaume and Meyerson had great difficulty with this problem.

Another type of the rotation problem was devised by Köhler. A stretched cord was fixed to a point outside of, and in front of, the cage. Its free end was lying inside the cage in such a way that the cord subtended an acute angle with the bars of the cage. On the middle of the cord, beyond the reach of the animals, a piece of food was fastened. To obtain the food the animals had to rotate the cord round the fixed outer point by passing the free end of it through the bars of the cage till in so doing the food came to a point from where it could be reached from within the cage. Curiously enough, here again lower animals often showed a better understanding than Köhler's chimpanzees. Two of these latter got no farther than a futile pulling at the rope, while three others solved the problem only secondarily, and only one found the right solution almost immediately. On the other hand, two monkeys of Trendelenburg, a pig-tailed macaque and a cebus of the author, as also two macaques of Verlaine and Gallis, found the right solution almost at once, and the same was the case with two raccoons and a coati of the author. With his lemurs the solution was less certain. Two gibbons of Guillaume and Meyerson were unable to solve the problem at all, and an orang not every time, whereas some lower monkeys and four chimpanzees found it directly. All this again proves that it is erroneous to suppose that in such problems insight correlates with the animal's place in the system. Lower animals often arrive at better solutions than higher ones, and the understanding is rather a matter of individual, than of specific, endowment.

The most striking cases of the understanding of causal relations by an animal are found, where it proves able to *use a tool*.

What is a tool ?

By a tool we understand an animate, or inanimate, object, not forming part of the body of its user, which temporarily is brought by an animal into its actions, in order to make possible, or facilitate, the attaining of some goal towards which it is striving. But we must at once add that the using of such a tool must not always be regarded as a proof of an explicit understanding of causal relations, as, curiously enough, the using of such tools sometimes occurs on a level on which there is not yet any question of such an understanding, viz., on *the level of instinctive activity*.

The best-known example of such instinctive using of tools in animals is found with the weaver-ant, Oecophylla smaragdina. These ants build nests of leaves of trees by sticking them together. For a long time it was not known how they managed it, as they do not produce any viscous substance. About half a century ago, however, it was discovered that they perform this with the help of their larvæ, which possess glands that produce a spinning substance able to be used for sticking the leaves together. In building or repairing their nests, the ants take the larvæ in their mandibles and move them to and fro from one leaf to the other ; while doing so, the larva disgorges a sticky secretion, which soon dries and thus holds the leaves together. The same behaviour, by the way, was also observed later in other species of ants.

These weaver-ants, thus, use their larvæ in two ways as tools : first as a tool to produce the sticking material, and then as a tool to bring it to the leaves. And even a third way of using a tool may be observed in them. If the leaves to be united are too far apart to permit an ant standing on one leaf to draw the other leaf towards it, a second ant comes and takes the first one in her mandibles and uses her mate as a tool to draw in the leaf. If necessary, chains of five or six ants may be formed in this way, the first ant standing on the leaf, while the last draws the other leaf in.

That we have here a case of the using of tools will not be denied. It was, however, not always clear how this behaviour had to be interpreted. Some observers were inclined to see in it an understanding of the result of their own actions by the ants, in other words, an intelligent using of tools. We cannot follow them in this interpretation. First of all, this behaviour is found with animals which show a highly-developed instinctive life but very little proof of real understanding. Again, the behaviour is not executed only by some very clever individuals but by all the members of the species, and is certainly innate, as is shown by the fact that even ants, removed from the nest when they came out of the pupa, showed this behaviour just like those living in normal conditions. It seems that the larvæ even assist in the weaving, in so far as they move their heads to and fro between the leaves. Still again, the larvæ themselves show a morphological adaptation to the behaviour of the perfect ants in their possession of spinning-glands, which are more developed in them than in the larvæ of related species, although they themselves do not spin a cocoon. Here once more we have an adaptation of the body of an animal to instinctive activity, of which we spoke in our second chapter, the more remarkable now, as here the instinctive activity of a perfect insect finds a correlate in a morphological structure of the larva. That a larva should have a morphological structure adapted to an intelligent action of an individual congener is, of course, unacceptable : that in these ants the using of their larvæ as a tool happens on the level of instinct, is therefore beyond doubt.

There are some more examples of such an instinctive using of tools by animals, although perhaps not so striking as that of the weaver-ants. It has been observed that some Ammophilas of different species used a small pebble to stamp the sand down the opening of their nest. The different observers of this fact disagree as to whether this was a performance of one special animal or was done by all animals of its species. If the latter be the case we may rightly ascribe the action to instinct. If only one, or several animals are found to do so, it would seem to be an example of individual intelligence. But then, perhaps, it may be ascribed to an old instinct of the species, yet living in other species, and in this species partly extinct but suddenly revived in one, or some, individuals. Other cases of an instinctive using of tools are the throwing up of sand by the ant-lion, if the prey tries to escape out of the pit, and the blowing up of drops of water by the fish Toxotes jaculator, which captures insects flying near the surface by shooting drops of water at them. And an interesting case was discovered a short time ago by Lack with the finch Camarhynchus pallidus of the Galapagos Islands. This bird searches for insects living in holes in the stems of trees, and to this end pokes into the hole with a little twig or a spine of a cactus and then throws it away as soon as the insect comes out. Since, according to Lack, all individuals of this species do so, there is again no reason to estimate this behaviour higher than an inborn instinctive activity.

But what interests us here are not the instances of an instinctive using of tools, but such in which the using of tools is built up upon an understanding of causal relations.

This intelligent using of tools may take place in two forms. Either the animal may *use a stick*, or something equivalent, *as a means to lengthen its arms*, or it may *use a box* or some similar object *as a means to lengthen its legs*, both in order to reach food laid down or suspended beyond its reach.[1] Let us begin with the stick.

The most common way of employing a stick is that of using it as a rake to rake food lying beyond the reach of the animal. In such a case the animal must understand that when it draws towards itself a stick it has laid behind a piece of food, it causes the food to follow the movement of the stick. We have already discussed as a precursor of this kind of free using of a tool the cases in which the animal draws in a stick the experimenter has laid behind the food. That much more is required from the animal, if it has itself to lay the stick behind the food, is proved by the fact that but few animals are able to do so. Whereas it does not generally occasion much difficulty to anthropoid apes to use a stick or some object with the same functional valence, e.g. a cloth, a bundle of straw, a water-bowl, a piece of iron-wire, and so on, as a rake, lower monkeys are usually not able to do so of themselves, even if they are able to draw in a stick laid by the experimenter behind the food. Yet there are exceptions to this rule : sometimes anthropoid apes fail, while by way of

---

[1] A few instances are known of the using of a tool by an animal in play. A chimpanzee belonging to Möbius took his water-bowl and struck back a nail driven into the wall of his cage, and a monkey belonging to Yerkes drove a nail into a board with a hammer. Chimpanzees belonging to Köhler used a stick in their playful fighting (but never in real fight !) and in play pricked chickens with sticks after first having lured them towards their cage. These, however, are exceptions ; generally the using of a stick as a tool is prompted by the feeding-instinct.

exception lower monkeys show the necessary insight. Here again the individual endowment of the animal is worth more than its place in the animal system. While gorillas and gibbons were nearly always lacking in the necessary understanding, the lower monkeys, especially some Cebus monkeys, were able to do so. A Cebus fatuellus of Klüver even used a living animal for this purpose. When a living rat on a cord was put into his cage, he threw the rat out of the cage in the direction of the desired food and drew the animal with the food in by the cord, sometimes waiting till the rat while walking round found itself behind the food ! In one exceptional case also it was reported that an elephant took a branch with his trunk and used it as a rake to rake in bread lying beyond his reach.

There are still other ways in which a stick may be used. Monkeys were sometimes seen to use it as a striking-tool, as a means to knock down food hanging above their reach. Sometimes the stick is thrown up towards such hanging food, although in this case it is not quite clear if this is done simply to hit the food or rather as an expression of the animal's desire for the hanging food. That sometimes the stick may be used to push food out of a tube has been mentioned above. Occasionally, apes used a little stick or twig as a spoon which they put into the water and then licked off. Köhler's chimpanzees used the stick to dig with, or as a lever to turn over stones. Chimpanzees and orangs, and even some lower monkeys, are reported to have used sticks as climbing-poles, which they placed under a hanging piece of food and along which they then quickly climbed up and grasped the food just as they fell down, stick and all.

The stick may sometimes be used also as an indirect tool. That is to say, if a piece of food lies outside the cage, and beside it, also beyond their reach, lies a stick long enough to rake the food in with, while a shorter stick lies within their reach, chimpanzees may use the shorter stick to rake the long one in, and then use the longer one to rake in the food. A Cebus of Cope drew in a strap he had lost with the help of a poker, and then used the strap to rake food in. That this roundabout way : "Short stick—long stick—food," is a method which the animals find difficult, is proved by the fact that even chimpanzees, who know how to use a single stick, are often unable to accomplish it.

The using of a box as a means to lengthen the body is more interesting than using a stick, in so far as in this case animals often do not stop after having drawn one box under the suspended food, but are able if necessary to draw a second or even a third box towards the same place and to put them one upon the other so as to construct a kind of tower. Placing a box under suspended food and mounting upon it in order to be able to grasp it, has been observed of many anthropoid apes. Instead of a box, a chair or a stone, or a roll or iron-wire, or a block of wood may be used ; chimpanzees of Köhler and Yerkes even tried to draw the experimenter under the food and to use him as a climbing-tool. Orangs and chimpanzees often showed themselves capable of this piling of boxes, although sometimes only after a period of trial and error. Some chimpanzees of Köhler and Bingham even got so far as to pile up four boxes. This has been the best performance known of animals. For technical reasons, but no less as a matter of insight, placing one box on another is far more difficult than simply drawing a single box under suspended food. The floor on which the animals walk, or lie, is the normal base on which they carry out their actions : the top of a box is a much less familiar plane, and it requires more insight to understand that this surface, too, may serve as a starting-point for placing a box than it is to understand that a box can be drawn or placed somewhere on the floor in order to be mounted. Added to this the building of a tower of two or more boxes is also technically rather difficult for the animals. Those built by Köhler's chimpanzees were often so shaky that the animals together with the boxes fell down when they tried to climb upon them. It was only owing to their finely developed sense of balance that they often succeeded in grasping the food before they tumbled down, together with the boxes.

In lower monkeys the understanding of the use of a box in order to obtain suspended food is not generally very well developed. As an exceptional case among lower monkeys a

Cebus of the author may be mentioned. This animal, after the experimenter had set it gradually more difficult tasks, was finally able to build a tower of three boxes. Among the lower mammals a dog of Sarris may be mentioned, who, when given a box mounted on rollers and provided with cords, pulled the cords so as to bring the box under a suspended piece of meat, while a coati of the author learned to do the same after a long period of trial and error. These, however, are exceptions. In general we may say that this task is too difficult for mammals lower than monkeys.

We may add that sometimes animals have been found capable of combining the use of a stick and a box, and so to integrate the two ways of using a tool into one action. Chimpanzees of Köhler sometimes piled up some boxes, placed a pole on them, and then climbed up the pole, or, standing on a box they had drawn under the food, used a stick to strike the food down. The same was done by the author's Cebus and a Cebus of Klüver. When Köhler once hung a stick high on the wall and placed a box in the neighbourhood, one of his chimpanzees drew the box under the stick mounted it, took the stick down from the wall and used it to rake in food. One animal, on the other hand, used a stick to draw in a box in order to mount it.

In this piling up of boxes a higher degree of intelligence is shown than in simply using an object as a tool. Here, indeed, the animal *not only uses a tool, but also constructs one.* In other cases animals were known to *improve their tools*, if these were inadequate for their purpose. Thus an oblong box may be turned up if lying on its side and not high enough for the animal. When the author's Cebus built a tower of two little boxes and a tin, he once missed the cover of the tin, so that it was difficult for him to stand on the tin. He thereupon went into the sleeping cage, came back with the lid he had left there, placed it on the tin, and then mounted it. Some animals which wanted a stick but could not find one, were able to make a rake for themselves. A chimpanzee of Köhler to this end broke an iron bar out of a boot-scraper and used it as a rake, or broke off a branch from a tree for this purpose. The same animal unrolled a roll of iron-wire

and used it as a rake ; others broke boards out of boxes, etc.
A macaque of Verlaine broke a twig off a plant, or pulled a
bristle out of a brush ; a Cebus of Klüver rolled pages of a
newspaper between his hands and the floor, and so made a
roll he could use. Objects used as rakes may also be improved
on if they do not satisfy. When a bundle of straw was too
soft to be used as a rake, one of Köhler's chimpanzees folded
the bundle into two and so obtained a shorter but firmer
rake. On the other hand, a chimpanzee of Guillaume and
Meyerson showed that he knew how to lengthen his rake
when he unfolded a foot-rule. And one of Köhler's chimpanzees, when two bamboo-rods were given to him both of
which were too short to reach the food, understood how to
put the smaller rod into the larger one and so to construct a
rake of greater length.

Now, it cannot be denied that all these performances
require a certain *imaginative faculty*, a certain phantasy on
the part of the animal. The animal must "see" the rake in
the bars of the boot-scraper, or in the branches of the tree,
while they still form part of that object ; it must "see" the
higher box in the oblong box on the ground, and the shorter
but more solid rake in the bundle of straw before folding it.
Some animals also showed that they were able to see in their
imagination objects, or parts of objects, wanted for the
construction of their tools. One of Köhler's chimpanzees,
when building a pile of boxes, went into the corridor to seek
for a box that he knew was standing there and which he
wanted for completing his tower, and the Cebus of the author
went for the same purpose into the sleeping-cage and fetched
the tin he had left there behind in play. Some imagination is
often shown even in the mistakes the animals make in their
performances. For instance, monkeys were often seen to lift
a box up in the direction of the food, or to press it against a
wall of the cage, as if expressing their understanding that if
the box could only be made to remain there, they would be
able to climb upon it and get the food. Even if the animal
simply picks up a stick in order to use it as a rake, or goes
to a box in order to place it under the food, some imagination
must be involved in this action.

Similar imagination, it may be said by the way, is shown by an animal in its play. If a dog treats as a prey a ball or a piece of wood thrown away before his eyes by his master, if he runs after it and catches it, shaking and biting it, just as he would do with a living animal, although he undoubtedly knows very well that this object is not a real prey at all, and, again, if in his playful hunting he alternately runs after his mate and lets his mate run after him, if in a sham fight he pretends to bite his playmate but does not really do him any harm, there must certainly be imagination underlying this behaviour, by which he harmonizes, but distinguishes, the playful case and the serious one. And must there not be some imagination in the dog or the wolf when he cuts off the path to the prey he is pursuing, a "seeing" of the prey at a place where it is not yet, but where it will be after some moments ?

These faint rays of imagination, shining on some of these higher intelligent performances of animals and their plays, lead us to ask the question, whether it is really true that the concrete understanding described in this chapter is the highest form of animal intelligence. May there not be something in the animal more like our own power of abstraction, like our thinking, like our more theoretical understanding ? Is there nothing in the behaviour of an animal to be regarded as a proof of ideation ? It will be our task in our next chapter to test the evidence of this as it is presented by the animals themselves.

CHAPTER VI

THE PROBLEM OF ANIMAL IDEATION

WE saw in our last chapter that the summit of animal performances in the field of practical understanding is the using, the improving and the constructing of tools. The question now, finally, to be considered, is whether there is or is not in the animal something of a more abstract nature than this understanding of concrete causal relations, something more akin to the higher mental faculties of man.

We have already credited the animal with some fantasy, which manifests itself in its play and sometimes enters into its intelligent performances. But does the animal possess *free images*, images free of what it perceives at some particular moment ? The dog may in his mind link the threatening whip with pain, and the particular spot in the field with the rabbit started there the day before. But can he, lying in his basket, ponder over the punishment he received from his master an hour ago, and remember the pain and the feelings he experienced during the punishment, or recall the walk with his master that morning and remember the pleasures he enjoyed then ? We may doubt it. If the monkey goes into his sleeping-cage in order to fetch a box he wants for building his tower, the image of the box to be found there is associated with the perception of the unfinished building. If he "sees" the rake in a branch of a tree, he really does see the branch at that moment. There seems no reason to credit him with more. Some will perhaps allege that the animal has free images during its dreams. That at least the higher animals dream seems very probable, although it will never be possible to prove this. The movements they make in their sleep, and the sounds they utter, resemble too much some characteristic movements and sounds of their waking life to be ascribed to accident or to casual reflexes of their body. Yet what we know about the dream-life of animals is so vague that it cannot give us any positive information respecting the images that pass through their mind at such moments and cannot even be regarded as a proof that any experiences really approximating to our dream-images actually occur in such supposed dreams. As proof of the existence of such imagery in the animals their dreams are of little value.

That animals do not form concepts, even such concrete and vital concepts as "food" or "water," as "mate" or "enemy," may be regarded as indubitable. If they did so, if they possessed such concepts, they would certainly have a word to denote it, a sound specifically meaning that object. The animals, it is known, *have no words*. All endeavours to train higher animals to use special sounds to denote objects in their world have failed. Animal language, if we may use the word "language" for the sounds an animal utters, is mostly no more than an expression of the animal's emotions and desires, uttered by the animal for itself alone, independent of the question whether another being hears them or not. Only rarely are these sounds intended to be heard by another living being as may be the case with animals living in a herd, or between mother and child, or exceptionally, as in the case of an animal like the dog, between animal and man. But even then the sounds uttered are inarticulate and innate, not articulated and learned in the course of life as is the case with the words of man. And even then, their sounds do not denote objects, but affections and desires ; they are not *indicative*, but *expressive*. The animal has no words, and therefore has no concepts, and as it has neither words nor concepts it is not able to do anything with them, to combine them, to manipulate them ; in other words, to think. Even the cleverest ape does not think while building his tower ; he does not say to himself : "Let me put one more box on the others and then I shall be able to reach the food." He simply sees what he has to do and does it. Such *seeing*, however, is not *thinking*.

Animals, thus, of themselves do not form concepts. Some experimenters have studied whether it might be possible to train animals to performances, for which some simple conceptions are required. Thus Hamilton placed his subjects (some normal and defective men and children, some monkeys, cats and a horse) in a space with four similar doors, one of which could be opened by pressing against it, whereas the others were closed. The position of the unlocked door varied irregularly from one trial to the other, with the proviso that the door which could be opened was never the same as the one that had been unlocked in the preceding trial. All that was expected of the subjects was, thus, that they should never try to open the door that had given exit the time before. Only the human subjects arrived at the understanding of this principle ; none of his animals (and a child of two years old) could discover it. They all tried the doors in an irregular sequence or, at the best, tried to open them in a succession one after the other. Révész placed four boxes before some lower monkeys and put the food successively in the first, the second, the third, and the fourth box. None of his animals was able to discover this simple principle of changing the place of the reward. Robinson, Klüver, and others, studied whether monkeys were able to form the conception "other than." In some of Klüver's experiments, for instance, four boxes were used, one of which was marked with a yellow circle, while the other three were marked with a blue one. Food was always put in the box which was different from the others, in this case, therefore, the box with the yellow circle. After the animal had learned to open this box, four boxes were presented, one of which was marked with an orange circle, the three others with a violet one. The monkey, then, in 97.5% of the cases opened the box with the orange circle. In other experiments his monkey had learned to choose a box with a black square in contrast to three boxes with a white square. Then, when four boxes were presented, three of which were placed at a distance of 100 cm. and one at 115 cm., this last one was chosen in 94% of the cases. But does all this prove that the monkey had formed the conception "other than," or "the only one of its kind"? We may doubt it. An object which in one conspicuous character differs from others always strikes us; so all that had been gained during the training was probably no more than to direct yet more the monkey's attention to the different element and to train him to choose this. That explicit conceptions like "other than" are required for this performance is not necessary; the whole process again may take place on the perceptual level. This is confirmed by the fact that the monkey in Robinson's experiment only gradually learned to choose the different box. Had he discovered the principle, had he grasped that he had to open the box "other than" the others, from that moment he should have made no more errors. But now the different only gradually obtained the valence of being the indicator of the place of the food. In all such explanations we must keep to the principle formulated half a century ago by Morgan, namely, that we must not ascribe an animal's action to some higher psychical process, as long as it is possible to describe it as the result of a process which stands lower in the scale of psychical development. If we relinquish this sane standpoint, all our explanations lose their power of conviction.

The animal, as we saw, is not able to form abstractions. But on the other hand it must be admitted that sometimes animals have proved to be able to perform something which may be regarded as a precursor to such abstractions, be it again on a lower level, viz., the forming of *perceptual generalizations*. Animals that were trained to choose a box which was marked with a triangle, and to disregard another one marked with a circle, afterwards also chose this box if it was marked, not with the triangle used up till then, but with some other kind of triangle, say a right-angled triangle instead of an equilateral, or a triangle with the apex downwards or to the left or right side, instead of upwards, or a triangle of different size or painted in another colour than that which had been used during the training. In such a case we must admit that the animal has grasped the sensorial generalization of "something with three sides and three angles."[1] To facilitate the forming of such generalizations it is advisable during the training period to change the triangle used from one trial to the other, as was done by Fields with rats. In one of his experiments, instead of the equilateral triangle, used up till then, a right-angle triangle was presented in eight different positions. His rats then chose it in 96% of the cases. Similar results were obtained by Buytendyk with a dog, and by Gellerman with chimpanzees. But in other circumstances, too, animals may give evidence of being able to form perceptual generalizations. If an ambulance-dog is trained to indicate "wounded" persons (i.e., lying) and to disregard "unhurt" persons (i.e., standing or walking), the dog must

[1] One danger, however, must always be kept in mind in such experiments. Animals sometimes train themselves, not to choose the box with the positive mark, but to avoid that with the negative mark, it being to this, therefore, that their attention is directed. If, then, some change is made in the positive mark, the animals may fail to notice it as it does not enter their consciousness with sufficient clarity. Before drawing conclusions, control experiments should be made to escape this trap !

have been able to form the perceptual generalization "man in a lying position," quite apart from the other characteristics of all these men and the way they are lying and in contrast to all other forms of human attitude and movements. But in these cases, too, the generalization does not overstep the perceptual level. The animal discovers the point of similarity in a number of partly-different perceptions, and learns to react in a particular way to this common element. But this does not pass beyond the level of the perceptual and we have no right to credit the animal with real concepts here either.

Does an animal *recognize* living beings or objects, known to it, on *pictures* ? The result obtained by the author with two monkeys were not very encouraging, although other experimenters seemed to obtain somewhat better results. But even then, if an animal reacts to a picture as before it had reacted to the object itself, must we admit that it really recognizes that object, i.e., that it understands that the picture stands in the place of the object represented ? Here, again, some doubt is permitted. If, for instance, a dog reacts in a hostile way to a picture of a cat or barks if he sees dogs running on a film, this, in our opinion, does not imply that he recognizes a cat, or his mates, in the pictures of them, but, on the contrary, believes he has to deal with real animals. If he had understood that it was only a picture, he probably would have kept quiet. The birds of Zeuxis in Pliny's story would never have pecked at the grapes in the painter's picture if they had understood that they were not real. The story may demonstrate that Zeuxis was a great realistic painter, but not that his birds recognized the grapes as paintings. I believe all such results testify rather to the poor vision of some animals, or at least to their inadequate use of their powers of vision than to their recognizing something as representing something else.

It is not necessary to continue these questions much farther. There is, we must conclude, a broad rift between animals and man. On the one side stands the animal, a creature living in the realm of the natural, the perceptual, the concrete only ; on the other side stands man, living also in the world of the spiritual, the conceptual, the abstract.

From the standpoint of evolution we must, of course, admit that man and the human mind have evolved from an ancestry mentally akin to animals such as are living now on earth. In the animal world, therefore, we are justified in searching for some indication of the higher faculties of the human mind. We may find perhaps a few faint traces, pointing to higher possibilities, abilities from which higher mental forms may develop. But we shall not find very much of this nature. Notwithstanding all similarity between animal and man in their instincts and feelings, there will in the mental sphere always remain a deep cleft between the two. For even at the apex of animal intelligence, this intelligence will never be more than *the intelligence of an animal*.

CHAPTER VII

THE PROBLEM OF THE ANIMAL'S WORLD

WHEN reading the concluding words of the preceding chapter, the reader will perhaps feel inclined to ponder what, then, is the world in which the animal lives ? Is it possible to get some idea of it ? Let us, in closing, try to form for ourselves an image of it.

When doing so, it must from the start be emphasized that the animal lives in quite another world than man, even if, as is for instance the case with our domestic animals, he lives in the same surroundings. First of all, as we have already seen in our two preceding chapters, there exists scarcely any *spiritual world* for him. The animal has no religious experiences, does not venerate a higher being, and even if he may feel himself inferior and submissive towards the leader of his herd or troop, or towards some human being, such a submission shows only a natural and not a religious character. He has no aesthetic feelings and does not admire the beautiful nor despise the ugly, even though he himself may, to our eyes, be beautifully coloured, or make constructions which we admire as beautiful. He does not conform to moral considerations and does not distinguish between good and evil, and even when he aids other beings, as for instance his young, he does not know that he is performing a good deed. He may be honest and may not be able to feign or lie, but is not aware of it himself. He has no sense of humour, and does not laugh, even if a dog or a monkey may sometimes grin as an expression of well-being. He has few free images, if any, and has only a few faint glimmerings of phantasy. The spiritual world of the animal is very poor indeed, so far as it exists at all.

His *intellectual world*, too, as we saw in the preceding chapters, is much more simply constructed than that of man. He does not possess concepts, and therefore cannot work with them, cannot manipulate them, cannot think, although he may find practical solutions for situations requiring understanding and insight. In this respect also he stands far beneath man.

On the other hand the animal certainly experiences the urge of his instincts much more than man does. His *instinctive world* preponderates over other inner experiences. The most important and ever alert of these instincts is that of flight. His whole life long the animal, at least the animal living in a natural state, is threatened by dangers and must be on his guard against enemies. Some few animals may enjoy a paradise on earth where they are free from all danger (for instance, the dwellings of men for his domestic animals and the Zoological Gardens for the few wild animals that have found a refuge there), but such paradises are exceptions. The animal in nature lives in constant danger, and this danger will impart a special colour to his world, unknown to most of us. Next to this instinct of flight the feeding instinct is the most important, while, at particular moments of his life, the sexual and parental instincts prevail. All such urges are undoubtedly experienced much more strongly by animals than by us, partly because they have so few other experiences to counterbalance them. The feelings aroused by these instincts, too, are for the same reason probably stronger than in man, at least in the higher animals, although on the other hand they are doubtless more elementary and much less blended with other emotions than with us.

Moreover, the *perceptual world* of the animal also differs greatly from that of man. Man is a visual being, that is to say, sight is his most important sense, the sense he depends on. His perceptual world is chiefly a visual one. As long as he is in a waking state his sense of sight is in action, whether he walks or works, writes or reads. Visual perceptions direct his actions. He acts much less on auditory impressions though these of course are operative, as when he moves aside for a motor car he hears behind him, or answers the questions of a fellow-man. The sense of smell plays only a subordinate rôle in his life. His perceptual world is in substance a visual one.

The perceptual worlds of animals not only differ from that of man, but are also different from each other. To start with, the order of the senses is different in different animals. In some of them the sense of sight plays the leading part, as in man, but in others the principal rôle is played by smell. The spider lives chiefly by feeling in a predominantly tactual world. Moreover, with regard to these perceptual worlds, we have to acknowledge that man is far from enjoying in all respects an unquestionable superiority.

Man is a visual being, indeed, but the visual world of many animals is richer and more differentiated than ours. Many of them, and not only the nocturnal animals but also an animal like the dog, can see better in the dark than we do. The power of vision of the bird of prey, which descries from a great height the prey moving on earth below, is greatly superior to that of man. Man's world is a coloured one, indeed, and in this respect is richer than that of many animals which are colour-blind, and live in a world of lighter and darker hues, like man's world in the uncoloured films of the cinema. This is, for instance, the case with most of the mammals : the dog and the cat, the rabbit, the cow. Of the mammals, only monkeys and apes have a colour-sense comparable with that of man. On the other hand, man does not see ultra-violet light as coloured, as is the case with the bee, which, however, by way of compensation, does not see red light as a colour, so that its visual world is shifted towards the side of the shorter wave-lengths. This does not render the colour-world of the bee richer, only different from ours. But it has been shown that some fishes distinguish no less than three different colours in the ultra-violet, while their red-vision is undiminished, so that their world is much richer in colour than ours.

The sense of smell is not very well developed in man, so that many animals live in a much richer osmatic world than we. This fact is well known in the case of mammals, especially the beasts of prey. Our dog, for instance, lives in a world of smells of which it is hard for us to form any adequate idea. Sniffing, the dog follows the track a rabbit has left in the wood ; his mates, and human friends, are recognized by him chiefly by their smell. It has been demonstrated that he is able to distinguish special smells when several are mingled, a task man cannot perform, as to us in a smell-mixture either one smell predominates, or a new smell is formed in which the components can no more be analysed. The dog, moreover, is able to recognize smells in a very weak solution ; for instance, iodoform in a dilute of 1 : 4,000,000, and sulphuric acid even in one of one to ten million. He is able to smell sodium chloride and quinine, substances odourless to man, and these even in weak dilutions. His retentiveness of scents is certainly much more developed than with us and he must have "smell-recollections" of persons and objects, just as we have visual recollections of them. It is not impossible, too, that his dreams are "smell-dreams," in which "smell-images" pass through his mind, just as our dreams are mostly built up of visual images. It also seems probable that to him human beings, and other dogs, have a "smell-physiognomy," i.e., that they may have for him a "malicious' or "good-natured" smell, just as for us persons may have a trustworthy, or unreliable, face, and that by emitting special scents that we ourselves cannot perceive, they convey their moods to him, so that the master "smells joyful" or "anxious" to his dog. The osmatic world of the dog is indeed of quite another nature than that of man ! Birds, on the other hand, do not seem to smell at all.

The acoustic world of the dog is also much richer than ours. His hearing is very keen. In experiments of Engelmann a dog could hear a faint noise (the falling of a small steel ball of 3 mm. in diameter on a steel plate from a height of 3 cm.) at four times as far away as did a man of acute auditory capacity. His hearing was thus 16 times that of man ! He also perceives, and can be trained to react to so-called supersonic sounds, sounds so high in pitch that the human ear is unable to perceive them. Many other mammals, too, have better audition than man, and can perceive higher tones. Recent investigations have shown that bats, when flying, evade collisions with objects by emitting similar supersonic sounds and using them for the purpose of echo-location.

Some lower animals, too, sometimes give proof of such acuteness of sense organs as we can scarcely imagine. When Fabre once let a female of the Emperor Moth Saturnia pavonia break out of the pupa in his room, in the evening about twenty males of that species collected round the wire cage in which the female had been put, and in a week's time he had in this way about 150 males in his house, although the moths were rather rare in his country and must have come from distances of several miles. And when Forel reared some females of Saturnia carpini in a room in his house at Lausanne, the number of males besieging his window was so great as to attract a crowd of boys in the street below. That it was the sense of smell which brought the males to the female was shown by Fabre with another species of butterflies (Bombyx quercus). When a female was put under a glass-bell in the room, the arriving males paid no attention to her, fluttering under the bell, but went directly to the place where the day before she had been sitting on the sand in a dish. Such attainments by the sense of smell are inconceivable to us.

Forel has pointed to the fact that in insects like ants and wasps the organs of touch and smell are situated together on the free movable and mobile antennæ. He therefore suggests that such animals may perhaps integrate their tactile and smell-perceptions into one complex perception such as to distinguish "round" from "square smells," etc., in the same way as man in his form-perception may integrate optic and tactile perceptions. This idea is perhaps somewhat fantastic, but, be that as it may, it must be admitted that such a capacity of building "smell-forms" would impart to these animals' sensory world constituents wholly differing from those of our own smell-world.

Have animals sense perceptions at their disposal of a kind wholly unknown to us ? This cannot be regarded as impossible, although it is naturally very difficult, if not impossible, for us to imagine such perceptions. It is known that some animals achieve very remarkable performances in finding their way back to their homes. Although many of the stories about dogs and cats finding their way home after displacement must certainly be treated with some scepticism, yet there have been some experiments, carried out with sufficient exactness as to be taken seriously, which have yielded surprising results. Bastian Schmid took a dog in a closed basket in a closed motor-lorry 20 km. along a road to a place 6 km. away, where the dog had never been before, and separated from the house by hills and woods. On being released, the dog, after a short period of hesitation, started in a direction almost exactly corresponding to that of his house and arrived there, although not in quite the shortest way, about one hour and a half later, having covered a distance of about 11 km. On a repetition of the experiment some weeks later he started after a few minutes in the right direction and arrived home in about three-quarters of an hour. What sense perception may have revealed to him the location of his house ? That migratory birds in spring often come back to the place of their former nesting after their sojourn in the South is a fact known to every bird-friend, although we do not understand how they manage to find this place again. Still more remarkable are the results obtained by Rüppell with birds taken by him from their nests and carried away great distances. To quote only the most astonishing among many other results, out of twenty swallows taken from their nests near Berlin and sent by airplane to Madrid and Athens, a distance of about 1,800 km., in seven days no less than four came back to their nests, two from each of the towns. How they were able to perform this is incomprehensible to us. The idea of some sense unknown to us intrudes itself upon our mind, although, it must immediately be added, the admission of such an unknown sense is a somewhat easy and cheap solution of a problem, and may therefore be used only if all other possibilities have been rejected with certainty.

It is clear, therefore, that the animals not only live in a world which differs vastly from that of man, but also that among the animals themselves the worlds they live in are quite different. Furthermore, we have to admit that there exist as many animal worlds as there are species of animals. The world of one animal will, intellectually and perceptually, be much richer and much more finely constructed than that of another. If it could observe and could appreciate such differences, the worm would look up as much to the ant as the chick would to the monkey. Generally speaking, the further one descends along the scale of animal life, the more the world of the animal shrivels. We saw this already in the preceding chapters with regard to the intellectual worlds. But the same holds true for the perceptual worlds. Where the structure of the eye becomes more primitive, the animal no longer perceives distinct images of its surroundings nor sees the forms and contours of things, but receives merely more or less vague impressions of them. At a low stage of development of the eye only the direction of the light is perceived ; at a still lower stage only differences in the intensity of the light, so that the animal merely distinguishes between light and dark, or perceives the changes caused by the movement of light and shadow. The visual world of such animals is of course much poorer than that of better equipped ones. In eyeless animals the whole light perception, if any, is based on the photic sensibility of the epidermis, as a matter of course much weaker than that of the eyes. That fishes do hear, a faculty much doubted, has been sufficiently proved of late years by von Frisch and his fellow workers. But among the invertebrates only a few insects really hear, so that for almost all lower animals the whole world of sounds is closed. Most animals are less sensitive to pain than we are, as is shown by the fact that foxes and rats sometimes gnaw off their legs when caught in a trap. Birds do not show any sign of pain when their wings are clipped and thereby their "hand" is cut off. Among the invertebrates pain does not seem to exist at all. An ant cut in two by Forel went on sucking honey as if nothing had happened. The chemical sense, too, disappears more or less in the lower orders. Probably only the tactile sense, the sense of being touched, is found throughout the whole animal realm. According to von Uexküll the whole world of the Medusa Rhizostoma, when floating on the blue waves of the Mediterranean under the southern sky, consists only in the perception of the rhythmical contractions of its own muscular apparatus. Whether this is quite true may perhaps be doubted, but it may serve as a good example of the poverty of the world of some lower animals.

Thus every animal lives in his own world, differing from that of other animals, differing especially from that of man. The knowledge of all these different animal worlds, embracing a knowledge of each animal's sensations and perceptions, of his feelings and drives, of his intellectual faculties and spiritual experiences, if any, must be regarded as the ultimate aim of the study of animal psychology.

BIBLIOGRAPHY

IN a volume of this size there is, of course, no place for a complete list of all the publications mentioned in the text. The author, therefore, believes he may restrict himself to naming some books of a more general character in the field of animal psychology, and for the rest refer to his "Tierischen Instinkte," in which a list of about 900 titles of articles and works on the subject of this book may be found.

J. A. Bierens de Haan. *Animal Psychology for Biologists. Three Lectures.* London, 1929.
—— *Die tierpsychologische Forschung. Ihre Ziele und Wege.* Leipzig, 1935.
—— *Labyrinth und Umweg. Ein Kapitel aus der Tierpsychologie.* Leiden, 1937.
—— *Die tierischen Instinkte und ihr Umbau durch Erfahrung. Eine Einfuhrung in die allgemeine Tierpsychologie.* Leiden, 1940.
J. H. Fabre. *Souvenirs entomologiques. Études sur l'instinct et les moeurs des insectes.* Série I—X. Paris, 1879-1910.
P. Guillaume. *La Psychologie Animale.* Paris, 1940.
F. Hempelmann. *Tierpsychologie vom Standpunkte des Biologen.* Leipzig, 1926.
R. W. G. Hingston. *Problems of Instinct and Intelligence.* London, 1928.
L. T. Hobhouse. *Mind in Evolution.* 2nd Edition. London, 1915.
H. S. Jennings. *Behaviour of Lower Organisms.* New York, 1906.
D. Katz. *Animals and Men. Studies in Comparative Psychology.* London, 1937.
H. Klüver. *Behavior Mechanisms in Monkeys.* Chicago, 1933.
W. Köhler. *The Mentality of Apes.* New York, 1925.
A. Kühn. *Die Orientierung der Tiere im Raume.* Jena, 1919.
J. Loeb. *Forced Movements, Tropisms, and Animal Conduct.* Philadelphia, 1918.
N. R. F. Maier and T. C. Schneirla. *Principles of Animal Psychology.* New York, 1935.
W. McDougall. *Psychology. The Study of Behaviour.* London, 1912.

W. McDougall. *An Outline of Psychology*. London, 1923.

G. de Montpellier. *Conduites Intelligentes et Psychisme chez l'Animal et chez l'Homme. Etude de Psychologie comparée.* Louvain, 1946.

C. L. Morgan. *Habit and Instinct*. London, 1896.

—— *Animal Behaviour*. 2nd Edition. London, 1920.

G. W. and E. G. Peckham. *Wasps Social and Solitary*. Westminster, 1905.

E. S. Russell. *The Behaviour of Animals. An Introduction to Its Study.* 2nd Edition. London, 1938.

E. C. Tolman. *Purposive Behavior in Animals and Men.* New York, 1932.

J. B. Watson. *Behaviorism*. New York, 1924.

R. M. Yerkes. *The Mental Life of Monkeys and Apes. A Study of Ideational Behavior.* Behavior Monographs, No. 12. New York, 1916.

G. Zunini. *Animali e Uomo. Visti da uno Psicologo.* Milano, 1947.

INDEX

INDEX

159

For Product Safety Concerns and Information please contact our EU
representative GPSR@taylorandfrancis.com
Taylor & Francis Verlag GmbH, Kaufingerstraße 24, 80331 München, Germany

www.ingramcontent.com/pod-product-compliance
Lightning Source LLC
Chambersburg PA
CBHW050526270326
41926CB00015B/3097